J 930.1 SCA
Scandiffio, Laura, author.
Digging deep : how science
unearths puzzles from the past

W9-BSE-618

DIGGING DEEP

HOW SCIENCE UNEARTHS PUZZLES FROM THE PAST

LAURA SCANDIFFIO

annick press
toronto + berkeley

Fountaindale Public Library
Bolingbrook, IL
(630) 759-2102

© 2019 Laura Scandiffio (text)

Cover art/design by Tania Craan
Edited by Catherine Marjoribanks
Designed by Tania Craan
Photo research: Mac/Cap Permissions

Annick Press Ltd.
All rights reserved. No part of this work covered by the copyrights hereon may
be reproduced or used in any form or by any means—graphic, electronic, or
mechanical—without the prior written permission of the publisher.

We acknowledge the support of the Canada Council for the Arts and the Ontario
Arts Council, and the participation of the Government of Canada/la participation
du gouvernement du Canada for our publishing activities.

Cataloging in Publication
Scandiffio, Laura, author
        Digging deep : how science unearths puzzles from the past / Laura Scandiffio.
Issued in print and electronic formats.
ISBN 978-1-77321-239-5 (hardcover).--ISBN 978-1-77321-238-8 (softcover).--
ISBN 978-1-77321-241-8 (HTML).--ISBN 978-1-77321-240-1 (PDF)
        1. Archaeology--Juvenile literature. 2. Excavations (Archaeology)--Juvenile
literature. 3. Archaeology--History--Juvenile literature. 4. Discoveries in science--
Juvenile literature. I. Title.
CC171.S23 2018   j930.1   C2018-904329-6   C2018-904330-X

Published in the U.S.A. by Annick Press (U.S.) Ltd.
Distributed in Canada by University of Toronto Press.
Distributed in the U.S.A. by Publishers Group West.

Printed in China

www.annickpress.com

Also available as an e-book. Please visit www.annickpress.com/ebooks.html
for more details.

To Rob, with love—LS

TABLE OF CONTENTS

Detectives of the Past

EACH TIME AN ARCHAEOLOGIST brushes the dirt off a remnant of the past, whether it's a pottery shard or a human bone, it adds a little to our knowledge. But sometimes an archaeological discovery is so startling, so unexpected, that it dramatically changes our understanding of history. It shakes up assumptions, overturns theories, and forces us to change our minds about what we *thought* we knew. Sometimes the new evidence is like a missing puzzle piece that, once put in place, changes the whole picture.

In the past century, stunning discoveries such as the tomb of the Egyptian pharaoh Tutankhamun and the Dead Sea Scrolls captured the imagination of the world. In more recent years, advances in science and technology have transformed archaeology, taking its detective work to a whole new level.

Thanks to radiocarbon dating, science can at last answer a question archaeologists have always wanted to solve—exactly how old an artifact is. Advances in extracting ancient DNA from bones means we can now reconstruct the genetic codes of people who lived hundreds or thousands of years ago—and know everything from their eye colors to their diseases. Now DNA can even link an ancient skeleton to a living descendant. With remote sensing—from radar and sonar to airborne lasers and satellites—it's now

possible to "see" through a jungle canopy, reveal a shipwreck at the bottom of the ocean, or map an entire ancient city from space.

And forensic science—all the technology available to crime solving—can be applied today to an archaeological site. The same science that detects the residue left from a smoking gun or determines the cause of a suspicious death is being used to reconstruct what happened hundreds or thousands of years in the past.

The true stories in this book are about recent discoveries that transformed our understanding of that past, whether two centuries or 40,000 years ago. And scientific breakthroughs made them possible.

A hidden cave in France proved that our Ice Age ancestors were more like us than we imagined—already powerful artists producing masterpieces. A skeleton found under a parking lot told a startling new story about a medieval king. A mysterious man, perfectly preserved in a glacier for thousands of years, became a unique time capsule of our prehistoric past. Ancient cities long lost under a jungle were brought into view, and the story of an empire's rise and fall was rewritten.

Today, archaeological finds are also playing a role in our planet's future—with discoveries that bear directly on climate change and a sustainable relationship between humans and our environment.

The stories of these dramatic finds are reminders that, despite our scientific advances, we still don't know it all (even when we might think we do!). There is still so much to learn about our world and our human story. Tomorrow, someone else might make a discovery that will make us question everything we believe today. It's what keeps archaeologists filled with a sense of wonder and anticipation!

> **WE ARE THE DETECTIVES OF THE PAST. AND WE HAVE TO FIGURE OUT WHAT HAPPENED. THAT IS WHAT IS FASCINATING ABOUT ARCHAEOLOGY.**
> —Luis Jaime Castillo, archaeologist

An archaeologist delicately removes earth from ancient human remains and artifacts.

5

Chapter One

ÖTZI THE ICEMAN

TIME TRAVELER FROM THE STONE AGE

HIGH ABOVE THE VALLEY, a man moves with strong strides up the mountainside. He is carrying everything he needs—food, fuel, weapons—in his backpack or wrapped in a leather pouch on his belt.

He advances steadily through the pines toward a mountain pass on the icy summit. His breath is steaming in the frosty air, but his animal-hide clothing keeps him warm. A couple of slain birds dangle from his belt.

It's clear he is in a hurry, retracing his steps downhill and then up again. What is he seeking so high up in the mountains—or fleeing from?

He will never get out of the mountain pass. The man's journey was made long before Stonehenge was built or the ancient Egyptians constructed their pyramids. And the answers to the questions of who he was and where he was going will lie preserved under the snow and ice for thousands of years—the world's oldest unsolved homicide case. When his secrets do come to light—thanks in part to advances in studying ancient DNA—they will also shatter assumptions about our early tools and technologies, the distances we traveled, and the diseases that plagued us even then.

The mountains and glaciers
of the Ötztal Alps

A GRISLY DISCOVERY

On a sunny September day in 1991, Erika and Helmut Simon, a German couple on holiday, were hiking high in the Ötztal Alps near the Austrian-Italian border. The scenery was spectacular, but the thin mountain air made their climb challenging. Veering off the marked trail, they glimpsed a brown object sticking out of the ice, which had partially melted in the sun. Coming closer, they stopped in their tracks. It was unmistakably the head and back of a person, dead and lying facedown. They thought it must be a mountain climber, recently killed in some tragic accident.

The Simons hurried down to the nearest mountain refuge—an hour-long trek—and told the landlord. The next day, police officers and volunteers returned to the scene and struggled to free the corpse from the ice, but they could not budge him. He was stretched over a boulder, in a peculiar position: his left arm under his torso sticking out to the right, his right hand stuck under a rock. They spotted strange items scattered around him, frozen in the ice—leather fragments, handmade rope. Not the usual gear of a mountaineer—who was this man? The skin looked oddly freeze-dried. The most striking object near the body was a long handmade ax with what looked like a copper blade.

Two mountaineers examine the mysterious corpse in the ice.

CARBON-14 DATING (RADIOCARBON DATING)

Carbon-14 is a variation of the element carbon that is present in all living organisms; it is steadily replenished as the organism consumes food or air. Once an organism dies, the carbon-14 in its tissues decays at a constant rate. So, by measuring how much carbon-14 is left in a dead organism, scientists can estimate how long ago it died. Thanks to this scientific breakthrough, archaeologists can date fossils and other remains that are as much as 50,000 years old.

Four days after it was discovered, the mysterious corpse was finally freed with ice picks. Without closer analysis, it was impossible to tell the age of the body, but one forensic scientist thought it could be as much as a hundred years old. Someone else thought it might be the body of a World War I soldier who became lost in a storm and froze to death. The corpse was placed in a body bag and flown out by helicopter, then taken in a hearse to the Institute of Forensic Medicine in Innsbruck, Austria.

A forensic examination of the body was carried out to identify the dead man and determine if the cause of death was suspicious. Early on in the exam, it became clear that the body might actually be hundreds of years old. The public prosecutor decided it was time to call in historical experts. Konrad Spindler, an archaeologist and historian, looked at the corpse and said it might even be 1,000 years old.

During the short time it had been out of the ice, the body had begun to deteriorate, so it was put in an icy cell. Samples of body tissue, gear, and plant remains found on the corpse were sent to three different laboratories for radiocarbon dating. All the results confirmed the same stunning revelation: this was the eerily intact body of a man who had lived 5,300 years ago!

The Simons had stumbled upon the oldest naturally preserved human body ever discovered.

The Iceman as he was found, lying facedown

A HUMAN TIME CAPSULE

Archaeologists and other scientists soon began to realize just how marvelous and rare a find this was. Ötzi the Iceman (as a journalist nicknamed him, after the mountain range where he was found) was so intact that he provided a unique window into the ancient world. Very few artifacts from Ötzi's era had been discovered in that region. No one knew for sure what our Neolithic ancestors were really like. Did they look like us? How did they spend their days? What did they eat and wear? Where did they travel, and why?

Nothing like Ötzi had ever been found before. His body and gear, perfectly preserved by glacial ice, were a time capsule of life in the New Stone Age—a turning point in human history.

How *did* Ötzi stay intact for over 5,300 years? He died at a high altitude, and over time his body was mummified by the ice, dehydrating his tissues and preserving them. Whereas Egyptian mummies were treated with special substances to prevent decay, this process happened naturally to Ötzi. A deep layer of snow and ice covered and protected this "wet mummy."

Archaeologists had to wait until the summer of 1992 to fully excavate the site. After removing snow and ice with steam blowers, they found even more clothing and equipment. They also turned up remnants of plants on Ötzi's body—pollen, seeds, moss, and fungus. All these held valuable clues about his diet, home, and travel.

Ötzi's arrows

LIFE IN THE NEW STONE AGE

The Neolithic Period, or New Stone Age, is named for the stone tools people used, made by polishing or grinding. This age began at different times in different places but started around 10,000 BCE and ended with the rise of the Bronze Age, between 3000 and 2000 BCE.

Our ancient ancestors once lived as nomadic hunters and gatherers, but in the Neolithic Period, people began to settle down in villages. They grew wheat and barley and raised goats and sheep. Population was on the rise, and people began to travel to trade with one another.

NEW STONE AGE PACKING LIST

Ötzi had been warmly dressed for the mountain wilderness.
His clothes were made of leather, animal hide, and braided
grass, stitched with animal sinews, grass, or tree fibers. He wore:

- a long coat made of goat hide, with the fur on the outside
- leggings made of goat and sheep hide
- a calfskin belt and pouch
- shoes made of deer hide sewn to a bearskin sole with
  the fur on the inside
- a bearskin cap
- a backpack, with a wooden frame and hide sack

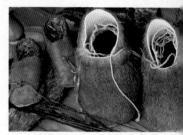

Recreations of shoes from Ötzi's
era, made of leather and fur.
String netting held in grass to
keep feet warm.

Ötzi's gear showed an ingenious use of plants and animal parts
to make everything he needed:

- two cylinder-shaped birch-bark containers, lightweight and tough
- a fire-starting kit—maple leaves wrapped around what would have
  been charcoal embers
- tools for scraping and boring and a piece of flint
- birch tree fungus, an antibiotic that could also be used to
  stop bleeding

The Iceman's unique copper axe

The Iceman was armed for encounters with wild animals,
such as wolves, or other humans with weapons such as:

- a longbow made of yew wood, still unfinished—the string had not
  yet been added. In an experiment, a replica of the bow hit targets
  30 to 50 m (100 to 165 feet) away with fatal accuracy.
- a quiver made from deer hide, containing twelve arrow shafts but
  only two finished arrows with flint arrowheads and feather fletching.
- a dagger with a flint blade and ash-wood handle. The blade had been
  forced into the handle and wrapped tight with animal sinew.
- a copper-blade ax with a yew-wood handle. The blade was fixed with
  birch tar and bound with leather straps.

New Stone Age weapons were
often made from wood, flint,
and tree fibers.

The unfinished bow and arrows were baffling—what was Ötzi doing in the mountains with weapons that weren't ready? But the copper ax was the biggest surprise for the experts. It was the only one of its kind found in the world, and it was extremely advanced for Ötzi's era. Experts had long thought that the technology to mine and smelt metal had appeared in Europe much later. Now they were forced to completely revise the time line of technology in the New Stone Age. Clearly, the people of Ötzi's time had already been moving beyond stone tools.

What's more, the copper in the blade was from hundreds of kilometers south. That meant people had been traveling and trading over a much wider area than anyone had thought. And the ax offered an intriguing clue to the Iceman's identity. In Ötzi's time, only men of high status would have had such an enviable weapon, one so prized it was often buried with them. Ötzi may have been an important man.

PIECING TOGETHER ÖTZI'S STORY

Scientists in Austria examined the body using X-rays and a CT (computed tomography) scan. They also made a few incisions to conduct a limited internal exam. Ötzi was then moved to his permanent home at the South Tyrol Museum of Archaeology in Bolzano, Italy. Glacier-like conditions of -6 degrees Celsius (21 degrees Fahrenheit) and 99 percent humidity were maintained at all times where the body was stored to keep it from decomposing.

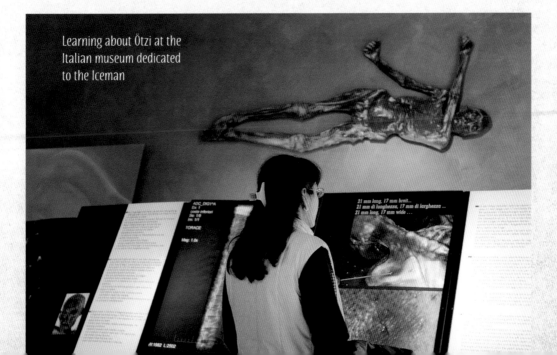

Learning about Ötzi at the Italian museum dedicated to the Iceman

TIME LINE

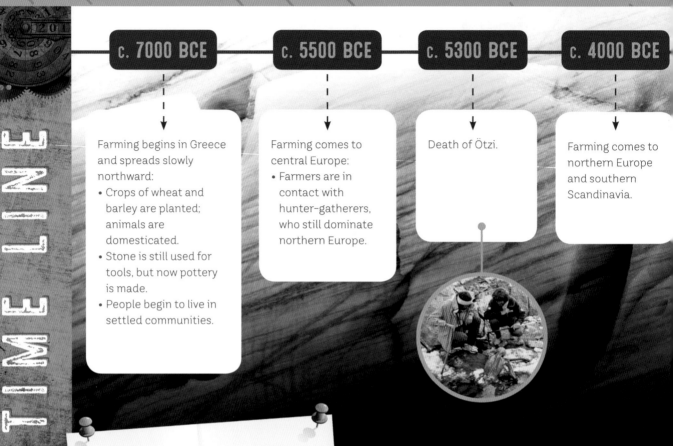

c. 7000 BCE	c. 5500 BCE	c. 5300 BCE	c. 4000 BCE
Farming begins in Greece and spreads slowly northward: • Crops of wheat and barley are planted; animals are domesticated. • Stone is still used for tools, but now pottery is made. • People begin to live in settled communities.	Farming comes to central Europe: • Farmers are in contact with hunter-gatherers, who still dominate northern Europe.	Death of Ötzi.	Farming comes to northern Europe and southern Scandinavia.

CT SCANS

Computed tomography (CT) scans work like a 3-D X-ray. A ring of X-ray detectors rotates around the subject, and a huge volume of data is processed by a computer that assembles the information into cross-sectional images (like slices in a loaf of bread). The result is a detailed, multidimensional view of the body's interior. In hospitals, CT scans help to identify internal injuries, tumors, and disease.

Slowly, scientists and archaeologists gathered evidence to piece together a theory about where Ötzi was from and where he was going. Chemical traces in his bones and teeth suggested he grew up in northeast Italy, perhaps in a valley not far south of the Ötztal Alps, and spent his adulthood in another valley southwest of where he was found.

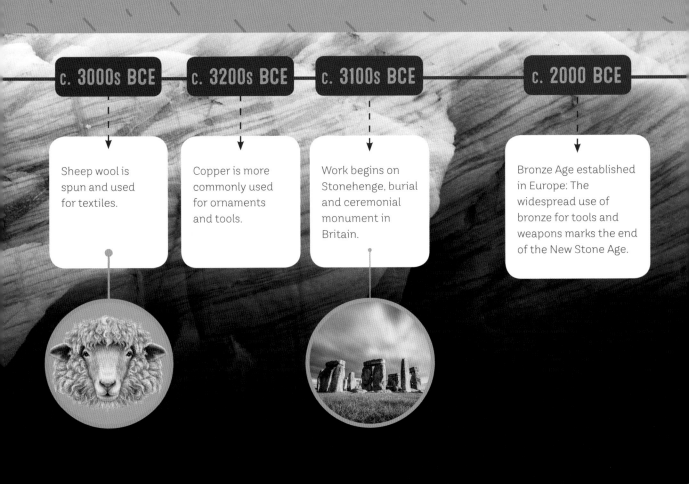

c. 3000s BCE
Sheep wool is spun and used for textiles.

c. 3200s BCE
Copper is more commonly used for ornaments and tools.

c. 3100s BCE
Work begins on Stonehenge, burial and ceremonial monument in Britain.

c. 2000 BCE
Bronze Age established in Europe: The widespread use of bronze for tools and weapons marks the end of the New Stone Age.

There was pollen in his intestine from two kinds of trees—one that grows at low elevations and the other high on the mountainside. This suggested he was on the move, up from the valleys to the mountains, in the time immediately before his death.

At first, researchers supposed he might have been a shepherd who took his flock to graze on the hillsides and got lost in a snowstorm. But there was no sign of wool or any other evidence to back up this theory.

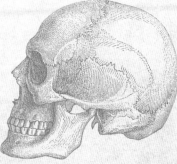

WHAT DID ÖTZI LOOK LIKE?

From the analysis, a picture of the man was emerging.

- **Age:** around 45, determined by a bone study
- **Height:** about 1.6 m (5 feet, 3 inches)
- **Weight:** about 50 kg (110 pounds); he appeared to be lean and fit, with strong leg muscles from mountain climbing
- **Hair:** dark, mid-length
- **Tattoos:** a total of 61 lines and crosses made by rubbing charcoal into incisions, all placed at acupuncture points, which scientists believe may have been intended to relieve pain
- **Injuries:** a slice across his palm that looks like a defensive wound, possibly from a hand-to-hand fight; broken bones and wear and tear on his joints revealed by X-rays
- **Other:** twelfth pair of ribs missing, a rare genetic condition

Could science reconstruct how the Iceman looked in real life? Using stereolithography—a type of 3-D printing—to make a copy of the skull, along with CT images of the body and all the evidence of his physical characteristics, two artists worked together to build a life-size reconstruction. Their Iceman replica was made of silicone rubber, synthetic resin, pigment, and natural hair. The result is startlingly lifelike.

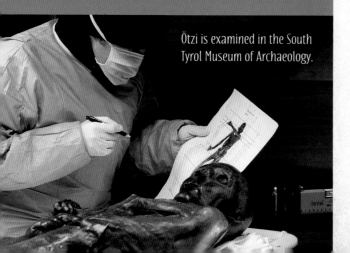

Ötzi is examined in the South Tyrol Museum of Archaeology.

AN ANCIENT MURDER?

Radiologist Paul Gostner continued to examine the X-rays, and ten years after the discovery of the body, he announced a startling find: a stone arrowhead lodged in Ötzi's shoulder. Its image on the X-ray had been mistaken for part of his ribs. Ötzi had been shot from behind. The arrow had severed an artery.

Strangely, the shaft of the arrow had not been found near the corpse. Did the assailant break it off and take it away after Ötzi fell? But then why did that person not also take the valuable copper ax? Researchers speculated that the killer might have been afraid that the ax would tie him to the crime, and it was too risky to be caught with it.

Was Ötzi killed by a rival? Had enemies fought him in the valley, then chased him up into the mountains?

Besides the arrowhead, Gostner spotted something else on the X-rays—the Iceman's stomach, which was pushed upward almost into his chest by the force of the ice on top of him. From its appearance on the CT scan, it seemed to be full. Did it contain the Iceman's last meal?

DEFROSTING THE ICEMAN

In 2010, scientists at the museum made the difficult decision to "defrost" the Iceman and conduct an autopsy. The danger of destroying him in the process was real, and they worked out a plan to limit the risk. Ötzi was removed from his climate-controlled crypt and thawed. Over the next nine hours, seven teams of experts—including pathologists, microbiologists, and surgeons—studied the Iceman.

The first team laid Ötzi in a specially constructed box to protect him from falling apart during the exam. Once the frozen tissues started to thaw, the body began to visibly sag.

An endoscope was inserted through one of the incisions made by the first researchers so the arrowhead could be observed on screen. But it was blocked by tissue. The surgeons had to decide quickly whether or not to make a new cut. Given that Ötzi was a unique cultural treasure, they decided it would be too damaging. The arrowhead would remain mysterious.

The next team stepped up to examine the brain. A CT scan had already revealed dark areas. Using pincers, the scientists reached through holes already drilled in the skull to extract small samples of the brain. Laboratory tests confirmed the presence of blood: that meant that Ötzi had received a violent blow to the skull just before dying.

Finally, it was time to view the stomach. The endoscope revealed that it was full of food.

Samples were extracted and identified as grain, meat, and fat. Ötzi's last meal included einkorn, one of the first grains humans cultivated. He'd also eaten the meat of an ibex, a wild goat that still roams the Alps. This was indeed a man who had lived at a turning point in human history, when people were just beginning to grow wheat but still living off wild animals.

A reconstruction of the Iceman shows how he probably looked in real life.

The final meal provided another clue. Food stays in the stomach for about an hour. This man had eaten a large meal shortly before he died. That didn't seem like something a man would do if he was on the run, fearing for his life.

So how did he die? Albert Zink, who directed the autopsy, put the clues together. Ötzi had been traveling with an unfinished bow and arrows, and he had been relaxed enough to stop and eat a large meal. It all pointed to one likely scenario: Ötzi had been killed from behind, shot in the back with an arrow, by someone he knew well enough to let down his guard.

And what about the head wound? There were two likely explanations. Either his attacker had dealt a fatal blow with a heavy object after wounding him with the arrow, or, after being shot by the arrow, Ötzi had fallen and struck his head on a rock.

Visitors view the Iceman reconstruction at the South Tyrol Museum of Archaeology.

After nine hours, the Iceman's body was stitched closed again. He was promptly returned to his icy cell and sprayed with sterilized water, which froze on contact. The examination had yielded 149 biological samples, which would be studied for years to come.

"ALL HIS SECRETS—INSIDE HIM, OUTSIDE HIM, ALL AROUND HIM—WERE OPEN TO EXPLORATION. ONLY THE ARROWHEAD REMAINS INSIDE HIM, AS IF HE'S SAYING, 'THIS IS MY LAST SECRET.'"

—Albert Zink

SECRETS OF THE DNA

Among the samples from the autopsy were tiny bits of bone. These would be pulverized in the hopes of extracting Ötzi's ancient DNA. The ability to decode DNA thousands of years old had recently improved dramatically—a great advance for science and especially for archaeology. Researchers had to hope that the DNA had not deteriorated.

INSIDE ÖTZI'S STOMACH: A HISTORY OF HUMAN DISEASE AND MIGRATION

Now that scientists are able to decode ancient DNA, another new scientific leap has been made possible: the reconstruction of ancient microorganisms that cause disease. Along with the human DNA extracted from remains, nonhuman DNA is also evident—usually bacteria.

Samples taken from Ötzi's stomach revealed the presence of a bacterium that is spread by contact. For this reason, researchers can use its presence to track the movements of human populations. In modern Europe, the bacterium is a hybrid of two ancient strains, one from Eurasia and the other from Africa. Yet Ötzi's is purely the strain from Eurasia. So people from Africa must have brought the bacterium to Europe during the last 5,000 years—much later than we thought.

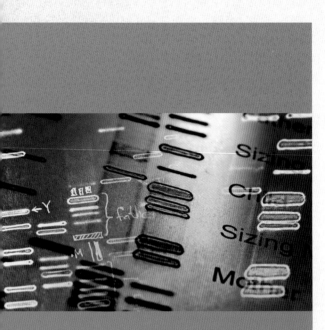

DNA: THE CODE OF LIFE

DNA stands for deoxyribonucleic acid, an organic chemical present in all living things—plants, animals, humans, and even viruses. DNA contains the genetic instructions for all our inherited traits. The DNA we share with our parents and siblings is the reason family members look alike. And our DNA holds information not only about ourselves but also about our ancestors.

In 1988, a team at Oxford University discovered that DNA could be extracted from ancient bones for analysis. Now it was possible to determine if a living person was related to someone who had lived hundreds and even thousands of years ago.

Ötzi had been perfectly frozen, which increased the chance of success, but he was also a "wet mummy," and high levels of humidity are harmful to the survival of DNA samples. People who had touched the body might also have contaminated it with their own DNA.

So samples from deep within a bone were sent to a lab to reconstruct a DNA sequence. It worked! Scientists could tell that Ötzi had brown eyes, had the blood type O, and was lactose intolerant.

They also discovered DNA belonging to a microbe. The researchers had found in Ötzi the earliest human case of Lyme disease. DNA also revealed that Ötzi had a predisposition to heart disease. The Iceman's DNA was opening another window into the past, this time changing scientific understanding of the history of human disease. Heart disease and Lyme disease, both thought to be modern developments, were clearly prehistoric—the genetic markers were there in our Neolithic ancestors.

There was another surprise in store: the Iceman's closest living relatives were not in the Alps but farther away on the island of Sardinia, off the southern Italian coast. Ötzi's DNA revealed that he was descended from farmers who had migrated from Turkey to Europe about 9,000 years ago. He also belonged to a genetic population group that is rare today—except in Sardinia, where people had been isolated enough to preserve the ancient DNA.

Ötzi does have more distant kin living today in the Alps, though. His DNA revealed a rare Y-chromosome mutation. When it was compared with 4,000 blood samples donated by Austrians, nineteen men were found with the very same mutation, and they lived not far from where the Iceman was discovered.

Every time we study Ötzi, we learn more about our New Stone Age ancestors. For one thing, they were more technologically advanced than we once believed. They were already mining and smelting metal to forge weapons and traveling and trading farther afield than we ever imagined, sharing knowledge and resources. And Ötzi has taught us about the beginnings of human diseases that we study and try to cure today.

The Iceman remains a unique link between our modern selves and our ancient past. Researchers have said that studying him brings him so much to life that they begin to feel sympathy for him. And knowing that there are people living today who share a common ancestor with Ötzi the Iceman seems to bring the past closer, so that we can look at our ancient ancestors and see ourselves reflected there.

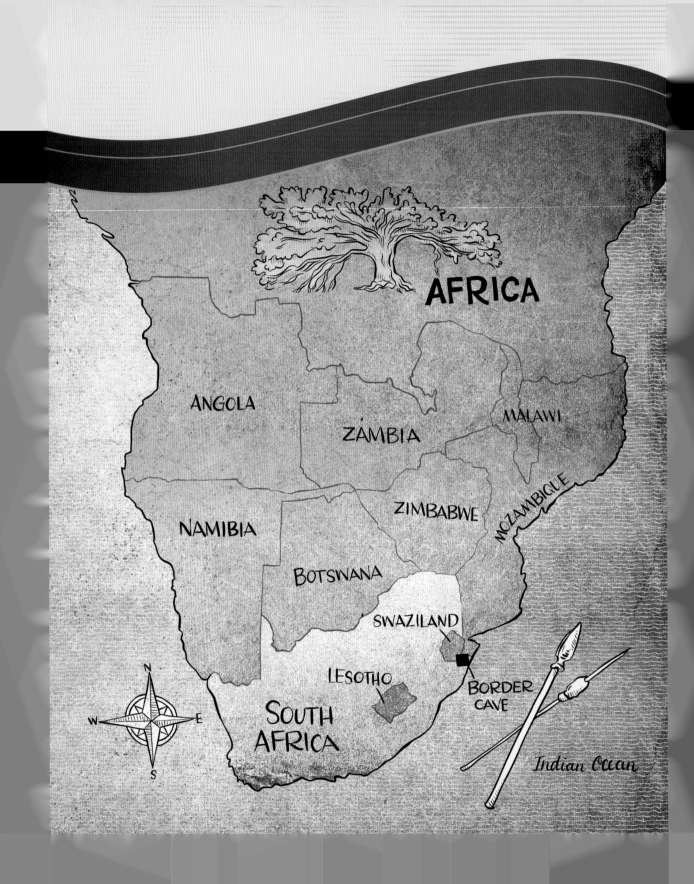

AFRICA

ANGOLA

ZAMBIA

MALAWI

NAMIBIA

ZIMBABWE

MOZAMBIQUE

BOTSWANA

SWAZILAND

LESOTHO

BORDER
CAVE

SOUTH
AFRICA

Indian Ocean

N

W   E

S

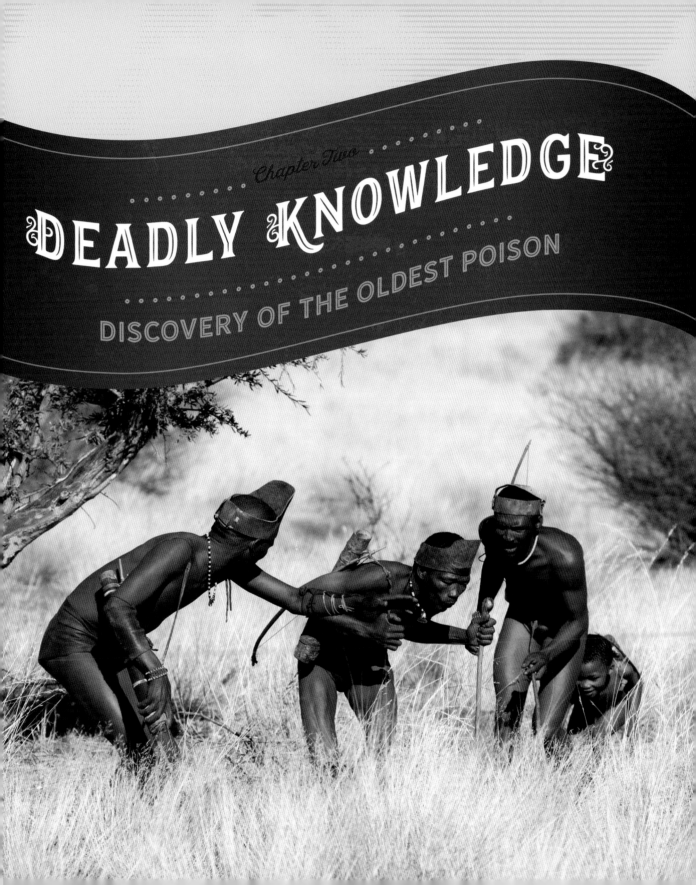

Chapter Two

DEADLY KNOWLEDGE

DISCOVERY OF THE OLDEST POISON

A HUNTER HAS BEEN FOLLOWING the tracks of a gemsbok, an antelope that grazes on the African savanna. Now he has his prey in sight and begins to stalk the animal carefully. The small hand bow he holds might not look powerful enough to stop the sturdy and swift animal. But he also carries an arrow with a secret: its slim stone point is covered with poison. He moves silently into shooting range; he knows he will have only one chance.

He aims and shoots. The arrow strikes its target, and its thin shaft falls on the ground. The antelope staggers; the poisoned arrowhead is still in its hide. The hunter continues to track the animal, waiting for the toxin to do its work and slow it down. At last the animal collapses, and the hunter can approach it and finish it off with his spear.

This scene might have happened thousands of years ago—or just decades ago. A hunter-gatherer people called the San, who live in southern Africa today, use tools and weapons—and poisons—that are a lot like artifacts from the Later Stone Age unearthed by archaeologists in Africa's caves.

A San hunter in Namibia

Anthropologists (who study human beings) and archaeologists (who study the material remains of the human past) have always been keen to pinpoint when tool and weapon making began. When did humans start attaching wood to stone to make spears? When did they move on to crafting the bow and arrow? And when did someone first have the idea to poison the tip? Modern science and technology would hold the key to many of the elusive answers. And what was discovered would change our ideas about the dawn of human technology.

SECRETS OF BORDER CAVE

Close to the border between South Africa and Swaziland, one cave has yielded amazing artifacts of ancient humanity. Evidence there of humans' extinct ancestors goes back 200,000 years. What archaeologists have found in Border Cave tells us that modern human beings very likely started out in the south of Africa.

The circular cave opens on a cliffside about 600 m (1,970 feet) up. It was first excavated in 1940. Going back through its layers of fossils and artifacts is like taking a journey through millennia all the way back to the Stone Age. Among the discoveries were:

Looking out over Swaziland from the mouth of Border Cave

- decorative beads made from ostrich eggshells
- pig tusks made into tools, probably used to shape and smooth wood
- bones with notches carved into them—were they used for counting?
- a thin bone point with a spiral groove filled with red ocher—much like the marks the San still make on their arrowheads

THE SAN—THE FIRST PEOPLE OF SOUTHERN AFRICA?

The San people are the earliest-known hunter-gatherers in southern Africa. Today, as in prehistoric times, hunter-gatherers collect wild plants, hunt, and fish. They don't farm, and their lives are nomadic, as they follow their sources of food. The San people use a unique weapon—a small hand bow and arrows with poisoned heads—to hunt their prey.

The San may be the closest living model for the hunter-gatherer way of life as it existed in the Stone Age.

In 2012, an international group of researchers led an effort to apply new technology to the cave's treasure trove of artifacts. Since the first discoveries at Border Cave, scientists had made important advances in radiocarbon dating (see p. 10). Now they could more accurately match measurements of carbon-14 in organic artifacts to calendar years and come up with even more precise dates.

Archaeologists had long believed that humans began to replace stone-tipped spears with the bow and arrow and developed more sophisticated tools about 20,000 years ago—a period in Africa known as the Later Stone Age. But now, thanks to the improved radiocarbon-dating practices, scientists discovered something very unexpected: the humans who had lived near Border Cave crafted tools and weapons like those of the San hunter-gatherers much, much earlier than anyone had guessed:

- A beeswax mixture wrapped in plant fibers was likely used for attaching bone and stone points to wood shafts. The new date placed it at 40,000 years old, making it the oldest human use of beeswax as a tool ever found.
- A digging stick, found to be 39,000 years old, was the oldest known artifact of its kind and looked much like the tools San women use to dig up bulbs and termite larvae.

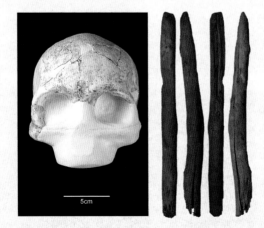
5cm

Border Cave finds: ancient human remains and tools

The new, more accurate dates did more than break records. Altogether, they told us that people began to adopt the technology of early modern humans 44,000 years ago—more than 20,000 years earlier than anyone had ever thought!

There was another surprise in store, as the finds took a startling twist. A thin wooden stick scarred with perpendicular scratches drew the archaeologists' attention. Chemical analysis showed traces of ricinoleic acid—a poison from the beans of castor oil plants. The archaeologists reasoned that the stick was used to put poison on arrowheads. At 24,000 years old, it was the oldest human use of poison ever found!

Archaeologists excavate at Border Cave.

LETHAL TRACES AND ANCIENT RESIDUES

Archaeologist Valentina Borgia was fascinated by the question of how long ago our ancient ancestors began to take poisons from plants and flowers and use them to make their weapons deadlier. "We know that the Babylonians, Greeks, and Romans used plant-based poisons both for hunting animals and in war," she explained, but the historical evidence did not reach further back than that.

Borgia began to research the many types of poisonous plants growing in different environments today, and she looked at how modern hunter-gatherers currently use them.

"Few hunter-gatherer societies remain today but all the groups that have survived employ poisons," she discovered. In the Amazon rainforest, the Yanomami people still use curare—from the *Strychnos* woody vine—to poison their arrows for hunting. In medicine, curare has been combined with anesthetic to relax muscles during surgery. But large doses paralyze the respiratory muscles, causing death.

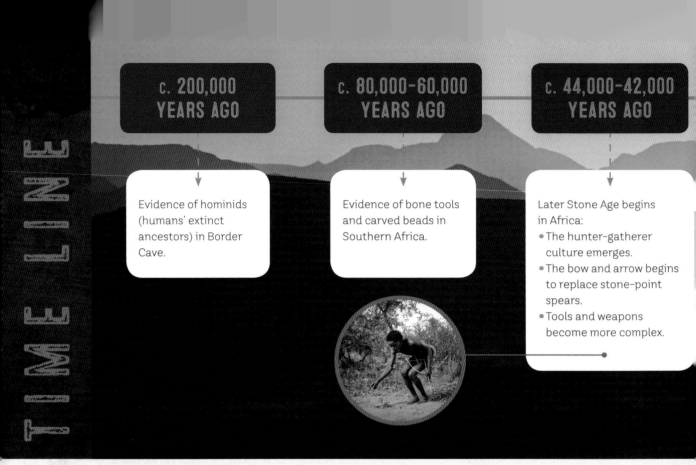

c. 200,000 YEARS AGO

Evidence of hominids (humans' extinct ancestors) in Border Cave.

c. 80,000–60,000 YEARS AGO

Evidence of bone tools and carved beads in Southern Africa.

c. 44,000–42,000 YEARS AGO

Later Stone Age begins in Africa:
- The hunter-gatherer culture emerges.
- The bow and arrow begins to replace stone-point spears.
- Tools and weapons become more complex.

Borgia was sure that ancient hunter-gatherers must have used poisons as well. After all, their stone arrowheads were probably not powerful enough to kill large prey. And they would have been familiar with the potential of the plants in their environments as food, medicine, or poison. It simply made good sense. She wanted to prove her hunch was right.

However, Borgia was an archaeologist, not a chemistry expert. In 2014, she enlisted the help of Michelle Carlin, a British forensic chemist who often works with Scotland Yard on criminal investigations to identify the invisible residue of illegal drugs. Carlin's method combines liquid chromatography and mass spectrometry. This two-part technique analyzes the chemical makeup of a substance, identifying the different chemicals present and their concentrations. Borgia and Carlin hoped this method, which could identify the merest trace of cocaine in a pocket lining, might also detect a smear of poison thousands of years old.

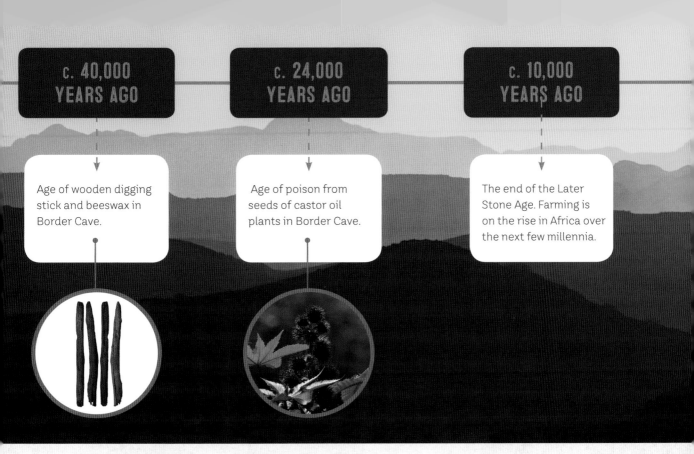

c. 40,000 YEARS AGO

Age of wooden digging stick and beeswax in Border Cave.

c. 24,000 YEARS AGO

Age of poison from seeds of castor oil plants in Border Cave.

c. 10,000 YEARS AGO

The end of the Later Stone Age. Farming is on the rise in Africa over the next few millennia.

THE POISON GARDEN

Their first step was to create a database of toxic plants whose traces they might expect to find on artifacts and collect samples of each for comparison. For this they visited the Poison Garden, located on the grounds of England's Alnwick Castle, which was used as the setting for Hogwarts in two Harry Potter films.

Visitors enter the Poison Garden at Alnwick through a black iron gate bearing a sign with a skull and crossbones that reads "These Plants Can Kill." Inside are over a hundred deadly plants, many of which are harmless-looking, even pretty, and commonly grow in gardens and parks. Foxgloves are planted for their lovely color, but their seeds are deadly. The fumes from cut laurel branches can make a person faint.

Some of the plants are so dangerous that a special license had to be granted for the garden to grow them. Visitors are warned not to touch, smell (or taste!) anything.

With the help of the Poison Garden, Borgia and Carlin compiled their samples of plants used through history for their lethal effects. Now it was time to test some historic weapons for traces of poison. And here they were in luck because the science to safely detect traces of poison on ancient weapons—without damaging the artifact—had only very recently been developed. Carlin was able to convince museum officials that she could use cotton soaked in pure water to remove a trace gently and harmlessly.

They started by testing artifacts that were roughly a century old. A Chinese pot was found to have aconite poison from monkshood inside, while Malaysian darts revealed the poison upas. Arrows from Africa bore traces of curare. But would their method work on something older—much older? Their next attempt was on 6,000-year-old Egyptian arrows at a museum of anthropology in California.

A stern warning at the entrance to Alnwick Castle's Poison Garden

Researchers had tried to test the black residue of the stone arrowheads forty years earlier. Back then, their method was to inject the mysterious substance into a cat. The cat survived, but the fact that it had difficulty walking afterward suggested that poison was present. Borgia points out that the cat test would have been a perfectly normal practice at the time: "At the beginning of the last century, scientists would even test substances on themselves and record how they felt."

> "POISON IS THE ANCIENT BASIS OF MEDICINE. FOR EXAMPLE, CURARE WAS USED AS A POISON BY SOUTH AMERICAN TRIBES, BUT ALSO USED AS A CURE FOR HEART PROBLEMS. IT'S ALL IN THE DOSE."
> —Valentina Borgia

POISON OR CURE?

Many of the same plants that have been used through history to kill can also be used, in tiny amounts, to heal.

Deadly nightshade: Its berries look like shiny grapes, but eating them is fatal. Another name for the poison is "bella-donna," which means "beautiful woman" in Italian, a reference to Venetian women who long ago used drops of its berry juice to beautify themselves by dilating their pupils (and risked blindness!).

Monkshood: It is popular in gardens for its unusual deep-blue flowers, which resemble little hoods. Every part of it is lethal, as the ancient Greeks knew. Small amounts were once used to bring down a fever, but with a large dose, a dropping body temperature and slowing pulse ended in death.

Castor oil plant: A helpful laxative can be made from its seeds, but the seed's husk produces deadly ricin powder.

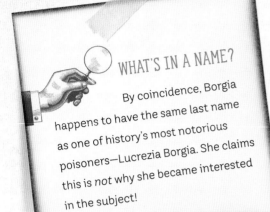

WHAT'S IN A NAME?

By coincidence, Borgia happens to have the same last name as one of history's most notorious poisoners—Lucrezia Borgia. She claims this is *not* why she became interested in the subject!

Euphorbia
x martini

Again, success: their first tests on the arrows suggested traces of *Acokanthera*, one of the poison plants in their database originating from North Africa.

Borgia believes that we now have the means to go even further back in time. By discovering what poisons prehistoric people used, we can trace their growing ingenuity, their knowledge of the environment, and, importantly, the earliest medicines they used. And another method of detecting prehistoric poison shows promise: looking for the starches they leave on weapons. Each plant species

TOP: Martin's Spurge, grown at the Poison Garden, is toxic if eaten.

BOTTOM: Visitors view the deadly plants at the Poison Garden.

has starch grains with a telltale size, shape, and structure. Borgia has appealed to other archaeologists to contact her when they find ancient weapons such as the ones at Border Cave. And not to brush off soil or wash them!

Our progress in technology has no doubt been less than arrow-straight: knowledge is gained, lost, and redis-covered. But the dating of artifacts in Border Cave tells us that humans were using inventive technologies in weapon-making at least 20,000 years earlier than we imagined. And one technology that our ancestors adopted much sooner than we knew was the use of poisons from their natural environment for hunting. This prac-tice allowed ancient humans to hunt more effectively, giving them a better chance to survive and the opportunity to move their culture forward.

Thanks to a leap forward in carbon-dating technology and the new ability to safely test ancient artifacts for tiny traces of invisible substances, we can now see the unbroken line linking our ancient ancestors with the hunter-gatherers—like the San—who still live today.

Hainan (CHINA)

THAILAND

LAOS

VIETNAM

•Bangkok

■Angkor

CAMBODIA

•Phnom Penh

Gulf of Thailand

South China Sea

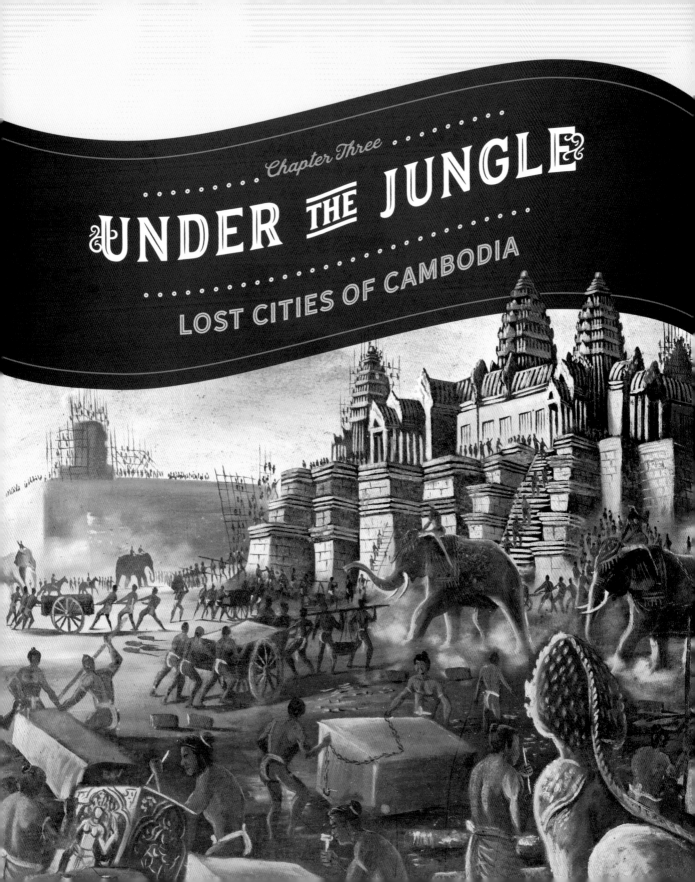

Chapter Three
UNDER THE JUNGLE
LOST CITIES OF CAMBODIA

IT HAS BEEN A LONG JOURNEY, by sea and through jungle, for the young man from China. His emperor chose him for a diplomatic mission to a faraway land. His name is Zhou Daguan, and he is eager to see what sailors have called "rich, noble Cambodia." After more than twenty-five days' travel, he nears the capital city: Angkor.

The grand city walls form a square, with a tower at each corner and five gateways, each one guarded by a pair of stone elephants. Surrounding the walls is a large moat, and each bridge that crosses it is lined with sculptures of deities. "They look like stone generals, huge and fierce-looking," Zhou writes for his emperor. At the center of the city is a tower of gold. All around, Zhou sees gold Buddhas and lions.

He is impressed by the wealthy, bustling city. The Buddhist monks wear yellow robes and shave their heads. The rest of the people tie their hair up in a topknot and wind a large piece of cloth around their bodies.

One day, Zhou catches a glimpse of the king as he comes out of the palace, something that happens only a few times a year. It is a huge procession. Soldiers and musicians are followed by hundreds of palace women dressed in floral robes. Officials and relatives of the king ride elephants. The king's wives and servants travel in portable beds carried by a person at each end. At last the king appears. He stands on his own elephant and holds the gold sword that symbolizes his rule. This may be a land of barbarians, Zhou muses, but it's one where everyone knows they have a supreme ruler.

The towers of Angkor in an illustration from the 1800s

After a year, Zhou sailed home and wrote of all he had seen. There would be no other eyewitness account until the sixteenth century, when a Portuguese traveler described an abandoned city, overgrown by the jungle, where huge tree roots sprawled over the ruins of once-magnificent temples.

What happened to destroy the mighty Khmer Empire? At some point, the Khmer rulers and their people abandoned their fantastic city, but why? Did war devastate the empire? Or was it something else? Did famine or a natural disaster play a role? Angkor's ruins stood silent witness to a catastrophe long past but offered no explanations.

The breakthrough in the search for answers would come with the help of a new scientific tool—one that could see through the dense jungle foliage to what was hidden beneath. It would uncover a whole new perspective on the culture, history, and technology of this Cambodian civilization. And it would pose the question: Was the empire's greatness also its downfall?

RUINED SPLENDOR

In 1858, Henri Mouhot, a French explorer, traveled to Southeast Asia. Mouhot had heard stories of magnificent sandstone ruins in the jungle and longed to see them. Mouhot and his guides trekked for hours, pushing through foliage and crisscrossing the winding river. At last they arrived at an open, level space with large flights of steps leading up to a platform.

VANISHED EMPIRE

Angkor was the capital city of the Khmer Empire, which at its height, from the late 800s to the 1200s CE, covered much of mainland Southeast Asia. Angkor's most famous monument is the Angkor Wat temple complex, built from sandstone in the 1100s CE. Angkor Wat is the largest continuously used religious monument in the world. Originally a Hindu temple, it was later consecrated to Buddhism.

Angkor Wat was the center of rites through which the Khmer king hoped to gain immortality by identifying himself with the Hindu gods. The temple complex has been said to represent the universe in miniature, as pictured in Hindu beliefs.

French drawing of Angkor's ruins based on Mouhot's sketches

The bustling metropolis Zhou had witnessed was now long gone. Mouhot marveled instead at the awesome ruins overrun by jungle and beheld the main temple of Angkor Wat for the first time. Over the centuries, Buddhist monks had kept the temples from being entirely destroyed by the encroaching trees. Viewing the remnants of this ancient kingdom, "grander than anything left to us by Greece or Rome," Mouhot wrote, "one is filled with profound admiration and cannot but ask what has become of this powerful race, so civilised, so enlightened, the authors of these gigantic works."

Mouhot's published account of his travels fired up the imaginations of European explorers and scientists, who longed to see these romantic temples lost in the jungle.

An aerial view of the ruins of East Mebon temple at Angkor

STRUGGLING TOWARD ANSWERS

In the 1860s, France established a colony in Cambodia. For decades, French archaeologists studied the Angkor area. They examined the pictures carved into sandstone and slowly decoded the inscriptions, many in Sanskrit, on the complex's pillars and walls. Gradually they pieced together clues about the Khmer kings and their religious and ceremonial temples.

But temple art and inscriptions are royal; they tell a story as the king wanted it told. Archaeologists wanted to know about ordinary daily life. What of the many thousands who had lived here? What had they been like? Where had they vanished to?

Only Angkor's temples, bridges, and canals were constructed of stone. People had lived in houses made of earth, wood, and thatch—materials that had rotted and disappeared centuries earlier, leaving little trace. Even the king's palace had been made of wood. Archaeologists wondered what clues lay beneath their feet, under the soil. Were there long-buried signs of these vanished people and their civilization?

A Buddhist monk walks among Angkor's ruins and the roots of giant trees.

To find out, they tried to survey the area on foot. Archaeologists hacked their way through the foliage with machetes, using handheld levels to map barely perceptible variations in the terrain that might be evidence of ancient buildings. In the 1990s, attempts were made to photograph the area from airplanes and then to map it with remote sensors such as radar. But most of the terrain was covered by a dense jungle canopy that even radar could not penetrate.

LIDAR

Lidar (light detection and ranging) is a method of determining the distance of an object by firing a laser beam from the air and measuring the amount of time it takes the light to bounce back and return to the sensor.

In a lidar survey, an airborne laser scanner (ALS) is mounted to the bottom of an airplane or to a helicopter skid. While flying over the terrain, the ALS pulses the ground with laser beams. The time the laser pulse takes to return gives the height of each data point on the ground.

The data is downloaded and calibrated, and then computer software creates a 3-D model of the terrain, including structures hidden by obstructions. Lidar has proved extremely useful in creating topographical maps.

LOOKING AT THE PAST FROM ABOVE

In 2012, Australian archaeologist Damian Evans proposed another tactic: looking from above in a new way, one that would cut through the foliage and make the invisible visible. His idea was to use a new technology—lidar.

In even the densest jungle, there are tiny gaps in the foliage where light reaches through. As the helicopter flies over the Cambodian jungle, the ALS would fire millions of laser pulses, many of which would bounce back off the trees. However, a small percentage would pierce the gaps and make it to the ground. The data would be collected and algorithms applied to filter out the vegetation. The result would be a 3-D model of Angkor showing only the ground. Lidar would be able to examine a much vaster area, much faster, than ground surveys. And since ancient ruins buried underground leave slight traces on the surface, lidar would detect the geometric lines of these human-made structures.

The mountain terrain north of Angkor in a digital image produced by lidar

Cambodian Archaeological Lidar Initiative   erc

Lidar could be a game-changer for investigating Angkor's mysterious past. The laser scanners would, as Evans described, "lift the lid and strip that vegetation from out of our view."

A VIEW TRANSFORMED

In April 2012, Evans led a research team to fly over the Angkor area. They timed it for the end of the dry season, when the trees had the fewest leaves. Evans's team mounted the ALS instrument in a pod and attached it along with a megapixel camera to their helicopter's skid. Taking to the air, they flew in a systematic grid pattern, staying 800 to 1,000 m (2,625 to 3,280 feet) above the ground to maximize accuracy.

In addition to Angkor, they flew over a remote mountain plateau to the north known as Phnom Kulen (Mount Kulen). Temple inscriptions hinted at a "lost"

> **IT REALLY IS QUITE AN EXCITING TIME TO BE . . . AN AERIAL ARCHAEOLOGIST LIKE MYSELF: SOMEONE WHOSE JOB IT IS TO LOOK FROM ABOVE FOR PATTERNS FROM THE PAST.**
>
> —Damian Evans

Ground Penetrating Radar and excavations reveal a more complex picture of what lies beneath Angkor Wat, including traces of earlier towers no longer visible.

41

Buddhist monks bless the lidar instrument before the flight begins.

SPACE ARCHAEOLOGY: NEW FRONTIER

Archaeologists, so often digging in trenches, have long dreamed of being able to take a wider view from above. In recent years, drones have proved useful in flying over excavations—where the view is clear—and taking pictures from a higher perspective. A drone can record in one hour what might take three months to achieve by a traditional ground survey, and its images can be used to generate 3-D models of structures.

Satellites orbiting Earth can map archaeological sites by detecting electromagnetic energy reflecting off the Earth's surface, invisible to the human eye. In that way, they can capture small variations on the ground, including ones caused by something lying beneath it. Now it's possible to pinpoint the location of an archaeological feature from thousands of kilometers away.

city there, even older than Angkor, called Mahendraparvata. While the city at Angkor embodied the Khmer civilization at its height, the lost city in the north represented its earliest days. Evans had a guess as to where it might be.

They waited impatiently for two months for the clouds of data points to be processed by computer. When the time came for Evans to view them on his laptop, he stared in astonishment. The model generated by the data was stunning. It revealed everything from large, landscape-scale imagery right down to incredible detail in centimeters. Geometric forms in the earth stood out with amazing clarity. Before their eyes, cities—where no one had expected them to be—sprang into clear view.

THE BUILDING BLOCK OF THE CITY

The wooden cities had vanished, but remote sensing revealed the clues they'd left behind. The archaeologists could now see the mounds of earth where wooden houses had once stood, high and dry in the wet season, and the ponds people had dug to hoard water in the dry season. Roads and canals had been laid out in a grid pattern. The city around the temple had been much more densely populated and organized than anyone had imagined.

One of the most striking features was the "neighborhood temple," which Evans called "the building block of the city." As he pointed out, "You can be standing right on top of one of these temples and not even know it." But from above, their horseshoe shape is easy to spot: a mound in the middle, surrounded by a moat, with a raised road on the eastern side. Remote sensing showed 1,000 of these small temples at Angkor, "each one the center of a community of hundreds of families, of thousands of people."

And the "lost" city of Mahendraparvata was found! A dream come true for an archaeologist. An intricate network of canals, roads, reservoirs, dams, and farming plots radiated from what must have been a central royal palace. "To suspect that a city is there, somewhere underneath the forest, and then to see the entire structure revealed with such clarity and precision was extraordinary," said Evans.

The discoveries changed our understanding of the early days of the Angkor civilization. The idea that early Angkor had been a simple and

Construction efforts reinforce and protect Angkor's delicate ruins.

unsophisticated society was completely mistaken. Not only had Mahendraparvata been a complex, organized city, but the people had already been expert engineers! There were signs of massive structures built to divert water to dry areas and to keep a steady supply of water during the dry seasons.

Evans suspected there might be even more out there. He wanted to extend the search, flying farther this time.

HIDING IN PLAIN SIGHT

Based on his success, in 2015 Evans led the Cambodian Archaeological Lidar Initiative. This time the team would fly farther, equipped with even better sensing power. While in 2012 they had covered 370 km^2 (143 square miles) in patches here and there, this time the lidar would sweep 1,910 km^2 (737 square miles).

Evans was right about there being more out there—much more. The 2015 flight revealed a dense, complex city that spread outward from Angkor's temple over at least 40 to 50 km^2 (15.5 to 19.3 square miles), connected by roads and canals to *other* cities.

Satellite image of Angkor area

"And this stuff had more or less been hiding in plain sight for a decade. We tramped all over this endlessly and just have been completely unable to see it or to map it," Evans explained. It seemed that everywhere they looked, old ideas were being overturned as each long-invisible city became visible again. The 2012–2015 discoveries were hailed by many experts as new evidence of the greatest empire on Earth in the twelfth century, once home to millions of people.

FROM JUNGLE TO MEGALOPOLIS

Lidar revealed that the Khmer civilization had been more advanced, much earlier, than previously thought. The Khmer people had re-engineered the jungle landscape on a scale rarely seen in the ancient world. It took sophisticated engineering know-how to keep the water supply consistent all year round.

Waterfall on Mount Kulen

Isla del Sol (Island of the Sun) in Lake Titicaca, Bolivia

SUSTAINABILITY: LESSONS FROM THE PAST

Archaeology—both on the ground and from the air—can help us to rediscover lost agricultural knowledge and may point the way to a more sustainable approach to the environment.

In Peru and Bolivia, modern farming methods have often failed. But aerial photographs and archaeological digs around Lake Titicaca revealed that around 1000 BCE, farmers' fields had been raised, built up with the earth dug from canals running between them. This was an excellent way to grow root crops, but the technique was apparently abandoned when the Incas invaded. When archaeologists reconstructed some of these ancient raised fields and planted root crops with traditional tools, the crop yields were much higher than in modern farmed fields, and they resisted drought, frost, and flooding.

A similar success took place in Israel's Negev Desert, where archaeologists rediscovered how farmers who had lived in the arid desert 2,000 years ago redirected water from cloudbursts into ditches and cisterns. Scientists were able to use this ancient knowledge to reconstruct farms that produce crops even in drought.

TIMELINE

| 790–835 CE | c. 890–c.910 | 1113–c. 1150 | 1181–c. 1220 |

↓

Reign of Jayavarman II. The Khmer (Cambodian) state takes control of smaller states and an empire is founded.

↓

Reign of Yashovarman I, who moves the capital to Angkor (the Sanskrit word for "city").

↓

Reign of Suryavarman II. Military campaigns conquer much of what is now Thailand. Angkor Wat is built and becomes Suryavarman's tomb.

↓

Reign of Jayavarman VII, who builds on a vast scale. The empire's territory is at its height, including modern Cambodia, Thailand, Vietnam and Laos.

The staple food of the Angkor civilization was rice, and those who grew it were at the mercy of variations in rainfall. In an ingenious solution, Khmer engineers took advantage of the natural flow of water from the mountains in the north and created a system to collect and store it in giant reservoirs—some were as big as 8 by 2 km (5 by 1.2 miles)! From the reservoirs, water was distributed to the rice

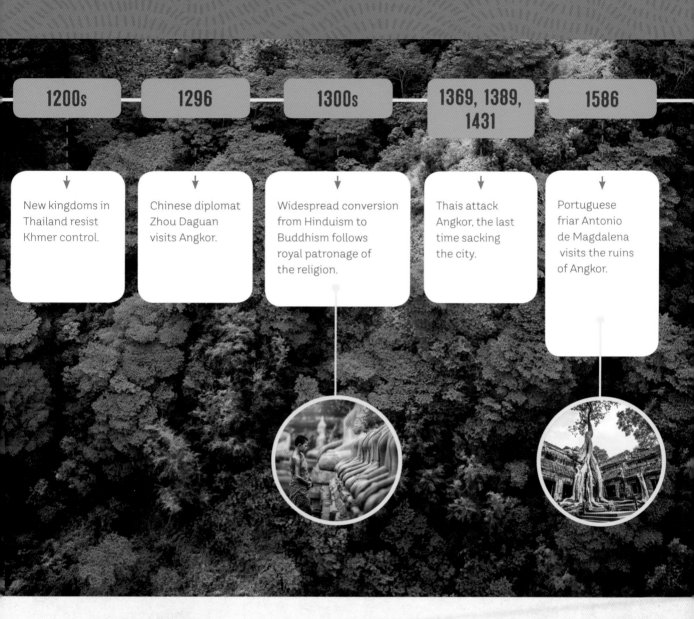

1200s	1296	1300s	1369, 1389, 1431	1586
New kingdoms in Thailand resist Khmer control.	Chinese diplomat Zhou Daguan visits Angkor.	Widespread conversion from Hinduism to Buddhism follows royal patronage of the religion.	Thais attack Angkor, the last time sacking the city.	Portuguese friar Antonio de Magdalena visits the ruins of Angkor.

fields by a system of canals, which also dispersed water during heavy rains. In this way, they both protected their temples and fields from flooding during monsoons and irrigated their crops during times of little rainfall.

AN EMPIRE'S RISE . . . AND FALL

The lidar results indicated that there was a dark side to this ingenuity. Thanks to Angkor's irrigation system, agriculture was so abundant that the population grew quickly. As the city expanded northward, all the building and farming led to forests being cut down, which must have brought problems with flooding and sediment in the water system. A breakdown in the brilliant irrigation system meant a disaster for food production.

Historians once believed that when Thailand invaded and sacked Angkor in the 1400s, they drove the king and the whole population south, ending Angkor's rule and ushering in a dark age. But if that were true, the lidar images would have shown newer cities built farther south—and none showed up. Instead, Evans has argued that Angkor's downfall resulted from the city-dwellers' reliance on the sophisticated water system and what happened when it degraded the environment. The engineering feat that ensured the empire's rise and spreading power very likely also brought about its end.

The magnificent temple complex of Angkor Wat

What we thought we knew...

and what we know now

The vanished Angkor empire has long been a mystery, a sketchy outline with many puzzling blanks. By aiming a revolutionary new technology at the old puzzle, we have come much closer to complete answers.

Whereas it was once thought that the Khmer cities predating the glorious capital of Angkor were simple, sparsely populated communities, lidar has revealed that they were in fact complex, densely populated, and sophisticated cities, existing much earlier than anyone believed. From its early days, this society had mastered the engineering technology to transform a jungle into a metropolis, to harness water in a complex system of canals and reservoirs to feed and shelter a growing population.

And the new discoveries strongly suggest that Angkor was not destroyed by a Thai invasion, but weakened by the Khmer people's own large-scale re-engineering of their environment. Mysteries remain for archaeologists to puzzle over, but lidar, by viewing the past from above, has allowed a giant leap forward in our knowledge of this ancient civilization.

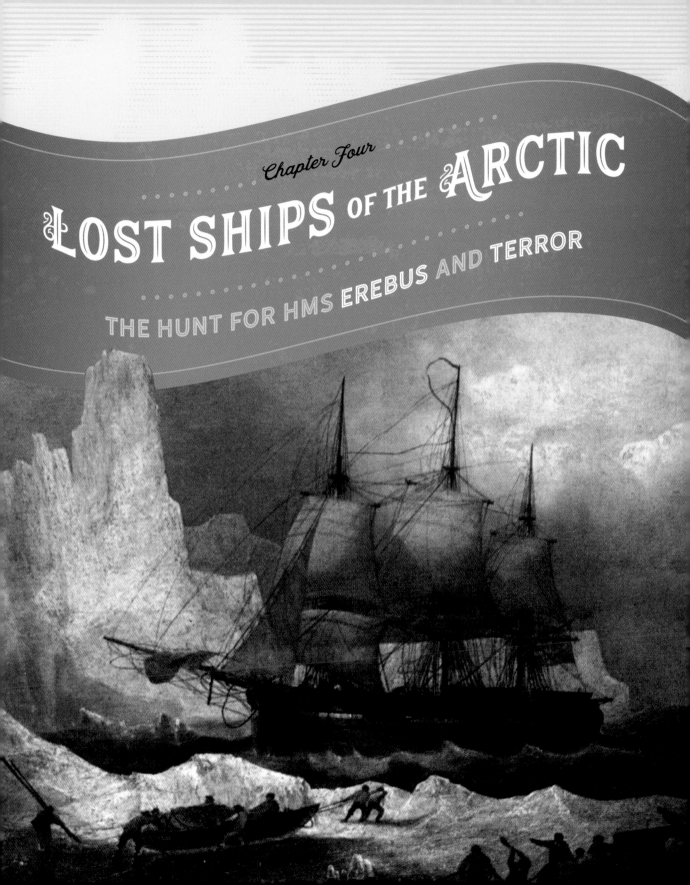

Chapter Four

LOST SHIPS OF THE ARCTIC

THE HUNT FOR HMS EREBUS AND TERROR

CHEERING CROWDS LINE THE BANKS of the River Thames. People jostle and stand on tiptoe for a better look; children are carried on shoulders to see over the throng. The focus of all the excitement is moving in stately progress along the river, towed by steamboats: two Royal Navy ships, HMS *Erebus* and *Terror*, their tall masts soaring high above their black hulls. They will wind along the river to the ocean, where they are bound for the Arctic on a voyage of discovery. Their commander, Sir John Franklin, is already a famous Arctic explorer, and he is seizing one last chance to reach for a prize that has eluded countless adventurers: finding the fabled Northwest Passage. To the people lining the river to watch, the Arctic is as far away and as dangerous a quest as going to the Moon.

In the months to come, something would go terribly wrong. Somewhere in the ice floes at the top of the world, the confident expedition would turn into a desperate struggle for survival. And the fates of the *Erebus* and *Terror* and their crews would remain a baffling mystery.

Beginning in 2008, modern archaeologists would take up the challenge to solve it, using methods both old and new. Along the way, they would make important progress toward understanding a critical threat to our own age: climate change—and the role the Arctic will play in our planet's future.

TO FIND THE NORTHWEST PASSAGE

Ever since the European discovery of North America, explorers hoped to find a shorter sea route around the continent to the Orient. Somewhere among the Arctic Islands, explorers believed, lay a passage of clear ocean to Asia.

Charting a Northwest Passage would be a huge boon to England's trade and naval power. In 1845, Franklin sailed from Britain with a crew of 128 men. He had been to the Arctic twice before, and he'd begged the Royal Navy's Admiralty for one last shot at finding the passage. Some thought he was too old, at 59, for such a grueling trek, but he had proved himself a tough sea commander. He had survived shipwreck, fought against Napoleon in the Battle of Trafalgar, and endured near-starvation while exploring the Arctic, when he became known as "the man who ate his boots."

Sir John Franklin

The Arctic as imagined by an English illustrator of the 1800s

This was the best-equipped expedition ever sent to the Arctic. Still, it was a perilous voyage to undertake. Icebergs, their massive bulk hidden underwater, could shatter a ship's hull. Ice and weather in the Arctic changed constantly; a ship could become trapped in ice that closed quickly around it.

Franklin's ships were seen by two whaling vessels off Greenland on July 26, 1845, near the charted opening to the Northwest Passage. One of the whaling captains wrote in his log that he had spoken to Franklin. The Englishman and his crew were in good spirits and all seemed well.

It was the last sighting of the *Erebus* and *Terror* before they vanished without a trace.

TO THE RESCUE

When over a year passed with no word, Franklin's friend and fellow explorer Sir John Ross volunteered to lead a rescue mission. The Admiralty turned him down. It was too soon to be alarmed, they believed. The expedition was well stocked with food.

After another year without news, the Admiralty at last took action. The search for the Franklin expedition became the greatest rescue mission in the history of exploration. At its peak in 1850, fourteen ships scoured the region at the same time, while overland searchers traveled by sledge. Navy officers, explorers, fur traders, and whalers took part. Ross was among them. That year yielded the first clues.

A search party had been combing the shorelines of barren islets when a sailor sped back to the ship and burst in upon the whaling master, Captain William Penny.

"Graves, Captain Penny," he cried. "Graves!"

Captain Penny and the other officers crossed the ice and scrambled up the rocky shore of Beechey Island. Three graves, identified with wooden markers, lay side by side in the permafrost, the only landmarks in a bleak expanse of snow. They bore the names of three young crew members. This must have been where the expedition

Drawing of an Inuit man by an English explorer

spent the winter of 1845–1846, in twenty-four-hour darkness. The sea ice had closed in for the season, and they had waited here for the spring thaw. But there was no clue as to why the three men had died.

In 1854, explorer John Rae spoke to Inuit witnesses and retrieved relics that could only have belonged to the men of Franklin's expedition, including silver spoons and plates engraved with the officers' initials. A harrowing story began to emerge. The Inuit, while hunting seals, had met about forty men dragging a boat and sledges by ropes across the snow and ice along the west shore of King William Island. The men looked thin. Unable to speak each other's language, they could only communicate by signs, which led the Inuit to believe that the men's ship had been crushed by ice and they were hunting for food. The Inuit sold them some seal meat. Later the same spring, other seal hunters found the corpses and graves of thirty or more people.

When Rae's news reached England, the Admiralty considered the case closed. Lady Franklin, however, refused to give up. After all, there was still no trace of Sir John, and even if her husband hadn't survived, she wanted to know his fate. She financed one last mission to discover what had happened. The *Fox*, commanded by Captain Francis McClintock, set sail in 1857.

A search party hunts for the lost expedition.

THE *FOX* ON THE TRAIL

McClintock discovered the first written evidence of
the explorers' fates on King William Island,
a desolate landscape of ice and stone.
Following Navy procedure, Franklin's
men had filled out a printed form
explaining their situation and
left it in a metal cylinder in a
stone cairn. The handwritten note
confirmed that the expedition had
wintered at Beechey Island. "Sir John
Franklin commanding the expedition. All
well." That had been signed by two officers
and dated May 28, 1847.

Objects from the lost Franklin expedition
discovered by early searchers

But nearly a year later, someone had
reopened the canister. This handwriting
looked hurried, crammed sideways on the margins:

> April 25, 1848—HM Ships Terror and Erebus were deserted on the 22nd April, 5
> leagues NNW of this, having been beset since 12th Sept. 1846 . . . Sir John Franklin
> died on the 11th June 1847, and the total loss by deaths in the Expedition has been
> to this date 9 officers & 15 men.

Mistakes were made about dates and the location of the cairn; were they signs
of mental strain and confusion? Then, scribbled in the top corner, upside down,
was a hasty postscript: "and start on tomorrow 26th for Back's Fish River."

So it would seem the crew had abandoned the ships trapped in ice, which had
never thawed over the summer, and then, after surviving two winters, had formed
a desperate plan to walk south out of the Arctic, perhaps to the nearest trading post.
But the English explorers, in their woolen coats and knitted mittens, were nowhere
near adequately dressed for such a trek.

McClintock spoke to Inuit witnesses who described a ship crushed by ice west
of the island. Other Inuit later spoke of seeing a ship farther south, with smoke
coming out. But it seemed the trail of clues had ended at the note in the cairn.

With that, the massive rescue effort drew to a close. Although the endeavor failed to find Franklin, it did advance the mapping of the Arctic. And there was one extraordinary accomplishment: while searching for Franklin by ship and on foot, Commander Robert McClure and his crew became the first to make it through the Northwest Passage.

But the *Erebus* and *Terror* had disappeared without a trace. What exactly happened to Franklin, his crew, and his ships would remain a mystery for the next 170 years.

AN ENDURING FASCINATION; A NEW SEARCH

In 2014, aboard the Canadian icebreaker *Sir Wilfrid Laurier*, Captain Bill Noon realized he had no ordinary command. "I think I have Franklin fever," he admitted in his online captain's log. He was referring to the obsession that has gripped so many historians and archaeologists to find out once and for all what happened on the doomed voyage. Perhaps the story continued to fascinate because it stirred people's imaginations. It called to mind human courage and recklessness and underscored the need to respect and understand the fearsome Arctic.

Canadian Coast Guard icebreaker *Sir Wilfred Laurier*

THE QUEST FOR THE NORTHWEST PASSAGE

T I M E L I N E

1534	1576	1610	1818-1833	1819-1827
French explorer Jacques Cartier discovers Newfoundland and navigates the Gulf of St. Lawrence while searching for a passage to Asia.	English navigator Martin Frobisher explores the Arctic for the passage and reaches Baffin Island.	English explorer Henry Hudson discovers Hudson Bay, but his crew mutinies and sets him adrift.	Expeditions by English explorers John Ross, William Parry, and Ross's nephew James Ross further the search. James Ross finds the position of the North Magnetic Pole.	John Franklin explores the Arctic overland and by sea and maps the coastline.

Captain Noon was part of a new mission to solve the Franklin mystery. It was a partnership among many groups, and the scientists on board would include marine and land archaeologists, hydrographers, and climate experts. Launched in 2008, its fleet included an icebreaker and a smaller, more nimble research vessel, along with underwater robotic vehicles and a team of divers.

This expedition was outfitted with technology earlier rescuers could not have dreamed of. Franklin's crew found their way with hand-drawn maps and unreliable

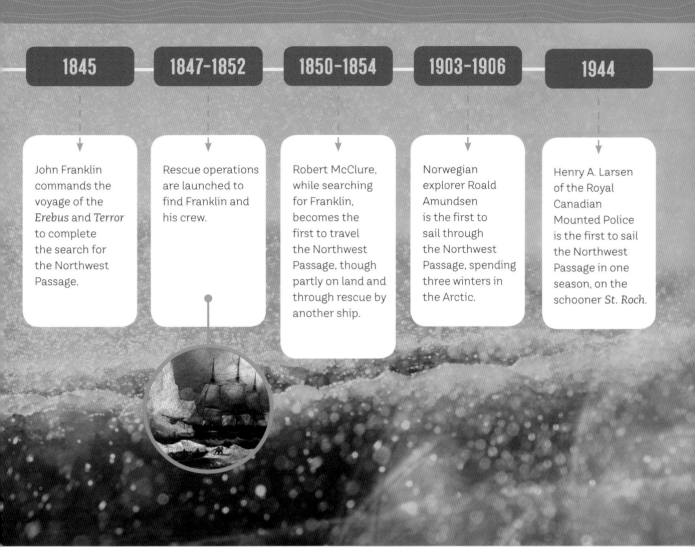

1845	1847-1852	1850-1854	1903-1906	1944
John Franklin commands the voyage of the *Erebus* and *Terror* to complete the search for the Northwest Passage.	Rescue operations are launched to find Franklin and his crew.	Robert McClure, while searching for Franklin, becomes the first to travel the Northwest Passage, though partly on land and through rescue by another ship.	Norwegian explorer Roald Amundsen is the first to sail through the Northwest Passage, spending three winters in the Arctic.	Henry A. Larsen of the Royal Canadian Mounted Police is the first to sail the Northwest Passage in one season, on the schooner *St. Roch*.

THE ARCTIC OCEAN: THE "WORLD'S AIR CONDITIONER"

About 30 percent of incoming solar radiation is reflected back into space by the atmosphere, clouds, and other surfaces, especially ice cover, which is more reflective than land or water. However, as climate change causes Arctic temperatures to rise, more Arctic ice will melt. As ice cover decreases, less solar radiation will be reflected and more will be absorbed. This raises global temperatures, which in turn melts more ice.

59

compasses, and they were hampered by ignorance of the surrounding land and ice. This time, communications equipment on the ship's mast would keep the crew in touch with the world. Their GPS (Global Positioning System) could pinpoint the ship's location in relation to any known dangers. Satellite images from space could be viewed on computers to help them track the ice flow; sonar would help them avoid obstacles that might damage the hull (see p. 66).

Although technological advances made the expedition less hazardous than in Franklin's day, the team still faced two of the same dangers: changeable Arctic conditions and uncharted waters.

SHIPWRECKED!

According to UNESCO, an estimated 3 million shipwrecks lie on the bottom of oceans around the world. Some are thousands of years old..

CHARTING THE UNKNOWN

The first task in the search was to chart the seabed. For much of the Arctic's waters, mariners were still relying on charts from the 1800s! As the sonar scanned the seabed, it produced detailed 3-D images of the seafloor. These were crucial to find the shipwrecks and at the same time created navigation charts, making it safer for ships to travel through the area.

This Franklin hunt combined modern technology with something much older: the Inuit oral tradition. The Inuit eyewitnesses of Franklin's day had recounted what they saw to their children, and the searchers were convinced that clues lay in the stories handed down through generations. Inuit storytellers carefully memorized and repeated details. Accuracy was a matter of life and death, since crucial information about ice or hunting was passed down by word of mouth. The searchers hoped that the tales about the sailors might have been remembered just as accurately.

A CLUE STAMPED IN IRON

The fleet returned each summer to hunt during the Arctic's brief window of opportunity, before the waters closed up with ice. In August 2014, the search was divided into two zones: one in the north of the Victoria Strait, close to the last known coordinates of the *Terror* and *Erebus*, and a second one farther south. The scientists were excited to unleash their best technological hope on the northern zone, a piece of military equipment called the Arctic Explorer. Built to find under-water mines, the bright-yellow cylinder operated like a programmed torpedo. Lowered into the water, it would swim off and use sonar to scan 2.5 km² (1 square mile) of the seafloor in an hour. When it returned, scientists could retrieve the images and view the bottom of the ocean in incredible detail on a computer monitor.

The Arctic Explorer was delicate, though, and vulnerable to ice damage. The team watched and waited for openings in the ice. Time and again they sent off the Explorer, but within an hour ice closed in, and they frantically retrieved it. The changeable and fierce Arctic climate was in charge. The ice that had wreaked havoc on Franklin now brought the modern search to a halt.

The search moved to the southern zone, where the ice had melted. The Arctic Explorer would be no good in the shallower water there. Instead, smaller boats with sonar units mounted on their hulls fed live data to the computers on the vessel. Underwater archaeologists took shifts watching grainy images of the flat seabed scroll down the computer screen, as sonar waves scanned the ocean floor. Still nothing. They were getting anxious. By September, the ice would be closing in once again.

ICE CORE: CLUES IN THE ICE

Climate scientists study past weather conditions by retrieving a long, cylinder-shaped sample of the deep Arctic ice. Like rings on a tree, the ice core displays a record of past weather. The evidence shows that Franklin's expedition took place during a series of extremely cold periods—the worst in 700 years!

Preparing the ice core drill

The search team explores the waters from the research and diving boat *Investigator*

Meanwhile, land archaeologists set to work on shore. Helicopter pilot Andrew Stirling flew an archaeologist and scientist to carry out their work on one of the small islands in the Queen Maud Gulf. Stirling, as usual, strolled the perimeter on the lookout for polar bears. Along the shoreline, a rust-colored patch among the gray rocks caught his eye. He knelt down for a closer look. It was a long, U-shaped piece of iron, about the length of his forearm. A broad arrow was stamped in the iron—it was the property of the Royal Navy!

A marine archaeologist compared the iron object to the blueprints of Franklin's ships. He soon had a match: it was part of a device used to raise and lower boats out of the water. This was the first solid evidence they had found, the most import-ant clue since the note in the stone cairn. The piece was very heavy, so it could not be far from where the ship went down. It fit in with Inuit stories of a ship farther south than the coordinates in the cairn, possibly with signs of life aboard.

SOUNDING THE DEPTHS

On September 2, the underwater archaeology team set out to explore the waters near the island with side-scan sonar. Ryan Harris watched the monitor on board, as images of a flat ocean floor scrolled down the screen. Then suddenly a new shape began to move into view, clear against the hazy background.

Before the entire image had materialized, Harris jabbed his finger at the screen and cried, "That's it!" The oval shape, unmistakable in its detail, was a ship. The ice that had forced them out of the more promising northern search zone had sent them straight to the right place.

The excited crew sent down a Remotely Operated Vehicle (ROV) to get a closer look and film what it found. The water was rough, the shipwreck covered in seaweed, but it was clear from the first captured images that it was in pristine condition. Its appearance and the presence of Royal Navy brass cannons convinced everyone it was one of Franklin's lost vessels.

A marine archaeologist examines the sunken hull of the *Erebus*.

A marine archaeologist takes notes on specialized underwater paper.

A diver explores the damaged hull of the *Erebus*.

Harris and another underwater archaeologist, Jonathan Moore, donned their cold-water gear and prepared to dive down and see it for themselves. Deep in the murky water, Harris followed the path of timber strewn on the seafloor, his excitement growing. "Then," as he later described it, "*boom*—towering out of the haze was this stately shipwreck."

About 11 m (36 feet) beneath the surface, it rose before him. The masts had been swept away, but the hull was in one piece, intact except for what looked like a large bite taken out of the stern. Holes in the deck allowed the divers to peek inside. Harris felt an immediate connection to the past and to the sailors who had once stood on this deck and slept inside these cabins.

Boys examine a small replica of the *Erebus* bell, made with 3-D printing.

Moore called Harris over to look at something else. Lying nearby amid swaying seaweed was the ship's bell. Embossed on its side was "1845," the year of the expedition.

Moore and Harris were careful not to harm anything. The artifacts were fragile after so many years in seawater. For now, they brought up only the bell—a symbolic artifact, especially to all the seafarers on the search. A bell is "the ship's heart."

The stamped iron fitting and the bell were strong identifiers. Exact measurements of the wreck from sonar data were compared to the original plans for the ships. They were a perfect match to the *Erebus*, the flagship under Franklin's personal command.

So the *Erebus* had sunk 160 km (100 miles) south of its last known position, in a protected area within a barrier of small islands. How did it get there? Did the ice finally give way, setting it adrift? Yet how could it have floated by chance through a web of islets to nestle in a bay? That seemed unlikely. Did this mean some of the crew had re-manned the ship and sailed it there?

And where was the *Terror*?

> **"YOU CAN'T IMAGINE HOW INCREDIBLE IT FELT WHEN, NOT EVEN HALFWAY ON THE SCREEN, THE SHIPWRECK EMERGED PERFECTLY RECOGNIZABLE."**
> —Ryan Harris

The remains of an officer's boot, recovered from the *Erebus*

THE SHIP "CRUSHED BY THE ICE"

In 2016, the searchers were back in the Arctic waters. Finding the *Terror* seemed like a long shot, as most experts believed it had been torn apart by sea ice and sunk deep in the ocean close to where the two ships had been abandoned.

Once again, a vital clue came from neither an archaeologist nor a scientist. A new Inuk crew member, Sammy Kogvik, shared an intriguing story. Several years earlier, he and a friend had crossed the sea ice on their snowmobiles farther north, in Terror Bay (named after the lost ship). Kogvik had spotted something tall sticking out of the ice, and the friends had stopped to look. It was a thick wooden pole. It reminded Kogvik of a ship's mast.

The rest of the crew thought the story was interesting enough to make a detour. They arrived in Terror Bay's uncharted waters early in the morning of September 3 and began to troll slowly, scanning the seabed with sonar. Kogvik tried to jog his memory, but everything looked different without ice and snow cover. After a few hours, they decided to move on. Picking up speed, the vessel moved out of the bay into deeper waters. Unexpectedly, a large object appeared on the ship's sonar display. It didn't look like a school of fish or a rock. Slowing down, they reversed course and passed over the same area for a better reading. The crew gathered around the screen and stared in awe as they passed over the digital image of a ship with three masts.

SONAR

Sonar (sound navigation and ranging) uses sound to detect objects underwater. It was first used to detect icebergs in an effort to safeguard ships. When submarine warfare emerged in World War I, sonar became an essential defense and was rapidly developed.

The sonar apparatus sends out sound waves that are bounced back by objects in their path. By measuring the time it takes for the sound pulse to return, the object's distance and direction of movement can be tracked. Sonar is used to chart the oceans, to measure the thickness of ice in the Arctic, to locate fish—and to hunt for shipwrecks.

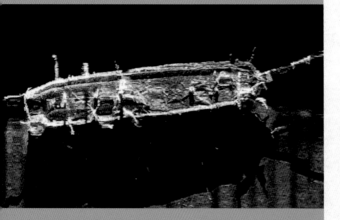

A side-scan sonar image of the *Terror* shows the wreck's excellent condition, including its masts and bowsprit.

Lowering an underwater camera and then an ROV, they took a closer look. The wreck was "sitting level on the seabed floor not at a list—which means the boat sank gently to the bottom," team leader Adrian Schimnowski later explained.

The ship lay about 24 m (80 feet) down in perfectly preserved condition. Even better than the *Erebus*! The whole of it was covered with sea life. But the hull was clearly visible, and the 6 m (20-foot) bowsprit was still intact. The masts were broken but still standing. Hatches were closed and everything neatly stowed.

An artist's depiction of the *Terror* trapped in ice

RAISE THE *TERROR*?

As pristine as it is, the *Terror* is unlikely to be raised from its ocean bed. In the past, shipwrecks have been raised and restored—for instance, England's *Mary Rose*, Henry VIII's flagship sunk in battle. But today, UNESCO's underwater cultural heritage convention advises that wrecks be left where they are found to preserve their historical context and the opportunities for scientific research.

As Schimnowski described it, "This vessel looks like it was buttoned down tight for winter and it sank. Everything was shut. Even the windows are still intact. If you could lift this boat out of the water, and pump the water out, it would probably float."

The team was able to precisely match their digital images to computer images of the original shipbuilder's plans. The second ship had been found!

The *Terror* was discovered 96 km (60 miles) south of where the ship was long believed to have been crushed by ice. Both abandoned ships may have drifted south and sunk, but this seems unlikely. Their course appears deliberate. By piecing together the wrecks' clues with Inuit stories, a more likely chain of events emerges. It seems the expedition did not all march south together; they may have broken up into smaller groups as they struggled for survival. One of those groups may have spotted the *Terror* floating free from its icy trap and returned to it, attempting to escape by sailing south out of the Arctic.

The ship's wheel, found still in place on the *Terror*'s upper deck

What we thought we knew...

and what we know now

For 170 years, people have speculated: What went wrong with the Franklin expedition? The three graves on Beechey Island led to the conclusion that illness had plagued the mission. Botulism and lead poisoning, possibly from canned food that had been soldered shut with lead, could have resulted in mental instability or erratic behavior. The bodies of the three buried crew members, preserved by the permafrost, were exhumed in the 1980s, and analysis confirmed the presence of lead. But it is unlikely that the reason for the disaster is as simple as that.

Experts generally agree that it is never a matter of a single thing going wrong in a failed expedition; it is usually a series of misfortunes. The crew's clothing was inadequate for Arctic survival. Illness may have worsened when they could not eat the food in the tainted cans. Added to that was a surprising turn in the weather. After a mild spring and a late season of clear sailing that may have lured Franklin to keep going, the explorers were likely trapped in a flash freeze-up. What followed was one of the worst winters in Inuit memory. It would become the stuff of legend.

Besides overturning beliefs about the fate of the ships, the discovered shipwrecks raise other challenges to accepted theories. It seems possible that the last survivors of the expedition did achieve their goal of finding the elusive link in the Northwest Passage.

As the wrecks continue to be studied, more information will come to light. It is still possible that somewhere underwater or in the permafrost, new evidence will be found—Franklin's log book or his grave.

The hunt for Franklin's lost ships has also enhanced our knowledge of the Arctic, its changing climate and unknown depths. Like the searchers of Franklin's day, we would do well to respect the Arctic's power and to understand its complex nature.

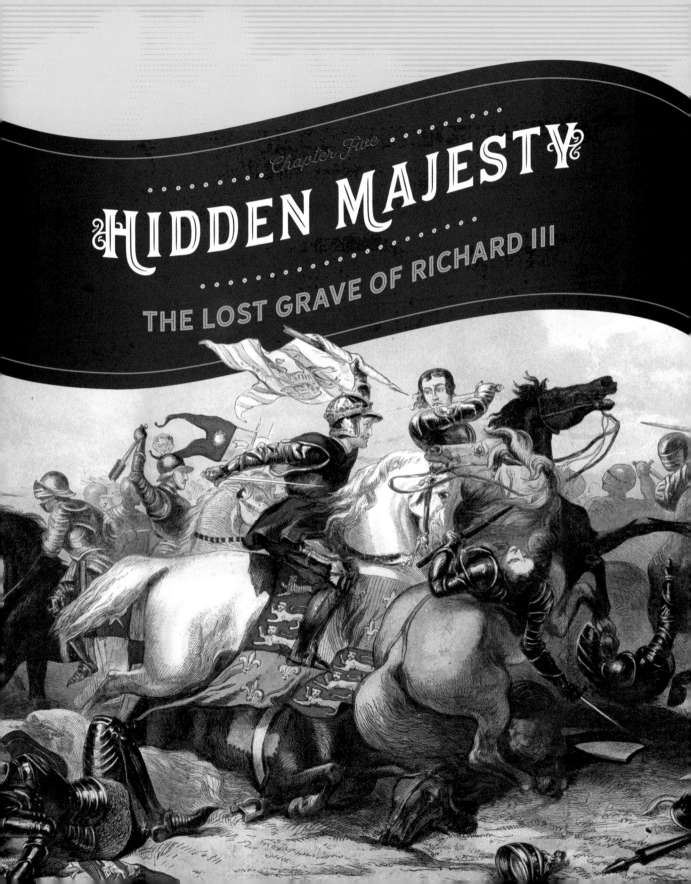

HIDDEN MAJESTY

Chapter Five

THE LOST GRAVE OF RICHARD III

ON A SUMMER MORNING, two armies approach from opposite directions. Soon they will meet in fields skirted by marsh in the heart of England's countryside.

The larger army pauses where it commands the higher ground, enjoying an advantage over the still-unseen enemy. Its leader is King Richard III. His opponent is Henry Tudor, a challenger for the throne, backed by an army of French mercenaries and Welsh supporters. Richard knows Henry's troops will come this way as they head toward London, and Richard's English soldiers will be waiting to intercept them.

Before setting out after dawn, the king paraded in armor on horseback before the line of his army, 8,000 strong, their banners fluttering in the breeze. He placed the royal crown on his helmet for all to see. It is a solemn ritual to symbolize his right to rule and to remind them of the loyalty they owe him. Richard knows that if he can defeat Henry today, he will destroy the only real threat to his throne.

Henry Tudor's army appears in the distance. It is much smaller, a little over 2,000 men. Henry is unsure of his chances and remains in the rear-guard, the better to escape should things go wrong.

The fighting begins, and the odds are in the king's favor. Then Richard does something as unexpected as it is bold. He gives up his place on the high ground and personally leads a cavalry charge, skirting the enemy army and galloping straight for Henry himself.

King Richard III on horseback
at the Battle of Bosworth Field

It is all over quickly. Richard is killed, the last English king to die in combat, at the Battle of Bosworth Field. Henry orders Richard's body to be stripped and draped over a horse and led to the nearest city, where it will be displayed for all to see and believe—Richard is dead, and Henry is now king.

This much was known to be true. But how exactly did Richard die? Where was he buried? Most important, were the terrible stories later told about this controversial king an honest portrayal? Historians puzzled over these mysteries for centuries. It was only with modern technologies—from DNA sequencing to forensic science and medical imaging—that the truth could be uncovered and a true portrait of a notorious king vividly painted.

> "AS FOR KING RICHARD, HE RECEIVED MANY MORTAL WOUNDS, AND LIKE A SPIRITED AND MOST COURAGEOUS PRINCE, FELL IN THE BATTLE ON THE FIELD AND NOT IN FLIGHT."
>
> —*Crowland Chronicle*

"HISTORY IS WRITTEN BY THE VICTORS"

Henry Tudor took the throne as Henry VII, and, little by little, the reputation of the defeated King Richard was destroyed. Chroniclers who had once praised Richard now condemned him. Did they at last feel free, now that he was dead, to tell the truth? Or was there another reason?

Henry VII undoubtedly had a strong motive to ruin Richard's name. His own claim to the throne was shaky—based on victory in battle rather than bloodlines—and he needed to strengthen it. One powerful way to do that would be to present

Henry VII

himself as England's savior, the king who overthrew a tyrant. Henry cast doubt on Richard's *own* right to the throne, claiming that Richard had staged a coup to take the throne from the rightful heir, his nephew Edward.

It has often been said that history is written by the victors. Could this explain what happened in the case of Richard III? Did chroniclers join a smear campaign to win favor with the new regime? If so, it worked extremely well.

With each retelling of his story, Richard became more villainous. He was blamed for more murders and crimes—all, apparently, part of his diabolical plan to seize power. The list of his alleged victims eventually included Henry VI; his brother George; his two nephews; his wife, Anne; and various nobles.

And what about his physical appearance? He had a crooked back, they said, a limp, and a withered arm. A physical deformity, medieval people thought, was a sign

In William Shakespeare's play, Richard III is a scheming villain.

of inner evil—or of God's punishment. The man was obviously a monster!

A century of attacks reached a climax in William Shakespeare's play *King Richard III*. His Richard is a hunchbacked schemer without a conscience, who kills for power and delights in his own wickedness.

A few people began to ask: Could Richard really have been *so* bad? Even his worst enemies had praised his courage in battle, and others agreed that as king he had upheld justice. Yet for the next three centuries, the image of Richard-as-villain stuck, and most historians accepted it. The real Richard seemed to be lost in a tangle of exaggerations, myths, and half-truths.

Even his grave had disappeared.

THE PATH TO THE THRONE

Richard III was born in 1452 and was King of England from 1483 to 1485. He was the younger brother of King Edward IV. When Edward died, the king's 12-year-old son was crowned Edward V. Richard took on the role of lord protector, running the government for the boy, who was too young to rule on his own. That same year, Richard brought forward evidence that his nephew was in fact illegitimate and therefore could not be king. Richard was crowned instead. Edward and his younger brother were sent to live in the Tower of London and eventually disappeared. It was long rumored, but never proven, that they were murdered by their uncle, the new king.

HOW DO YOU LOSE A KING'S GRAVE?

It is surprising and bizarre—how *could* the grave of someone as important as a king get lost? Accounts written in the first years after Richard's death are sketchy, but it seems that for two or three days his corpse was displayed publicly in Leicester, the city nearest the battlefield. This was on Henry's orders, to prove Richard was dead. Richard was then buried "without any pomp or solemn funeral"—dropped into a hastily dug pit—in the floor of a local church. Two later accounts confirmed this was in the church of the "Greyfriars," friars who wore gray robes.

In the 1500s, during a period of religious upheaval in England, many churches were destroyed, including the Greyfriars priory. A story began to circulate that, in the turmoil, Richard's remains had been dug up. An angry mob had carried his body through the streets and dumped it into the river. In the 1600s, historian John Speede wrote that Richard's now-empty gravesite was in ruins, and his stone coffin had been made into a drinking trough for horses. Most historians accepted this account. There was no evidence to refute it.

In the centuries that followed, new buildings rose over the ruins of old ones, and the medieval city vanished beneath them. And with it disappeared any certainty about where Richard's final remains might be.

AN ANCIENT MAP AND A DNA SEQUENCE

In 2004, English historian John Ashdown-Hill took a closer look at Speede's account of searching for Richard's grave and the map he had drawn. He discovered that Speede had made a mistake: he had gone to the site of the Blackfriars priory, not the Greyfriars! Could Richard's remains still lie somewhere under modern Leicester?

At the same time, Ashdown-Hill had been asked to help identify a set of bones buried in a Belgian church. They might be the remains of Richard's sister Margaret of York. Could he produce a DNA sequence for Margaret to confirm it was her? To do this, he would need a DNA sample from one of her descendants. First, he would have to trace a family tree, mother to daughter, to a living descendant of Margaret's. Technology was now available to compare that person's DNA with the DNA of the skeletal remains and see if they matched (see p. 20).

Margaret's family tree died out, so Ashdown-Hill tried again with Richard's older sister Anne. He scoured baptismal registers, census data, and family letters. To his growing amazement, the line kept going, mother to daughter. Richard's sixteenth grandniece was living in Canada—Joy Ibsen. When Ashdown-Hill contacted Ibsen with the news, she was stunned. She had no idea she was related to the infamous king.

King Richard III

Richard had no direct descendants. But Ashdown-Hill realized that just as a mtDNA match with Ibsen could prove that the skeleton in Belgium was Margaret's, it could also prove the identity of Richard's remains—if only his lost burial place could be found.

AN EERIE INTUITION

Philippa Langley, a writer living in Edinburgh, was visiting Leicester in 2004 to get ideas for a screenplay. She believed history had been unfair to Richard III and that his life would make a dramatic movie. Maybe walking the streets of the city he visited before his final battle would provide inspiration.

mtDNA

Our cells contain two types of DNA. Nuclear DNA is a fifty-fifty mixture of both parents' DNA. But mitochondrial DNA (mtDNA) is inherited entirely from the mother unchanged. Richard and his sisters would have had identical mtDNA, inherited from their mother. Yet only his sisters would pass on that mtDNA to their children, and only their daughters could pass it on in turn.

Langley headed to a parking lot on New Street. A portion of a ruined medieval wall in the modern car park had prompted rumors that the Greyfriars church might have once stood there. She walked past the cars to the stone wall, but nothing seemed helpful to her quest. As she exited, she noticed another parking lot across the street, behind gates and a "Private" sign. Curious, she slipped through and walked across the lot toward a red brick wall at the other end.

As she neared the wall she felt the oddest sensation: "My heart was pounding . . . I had goose bumps, so much so that even in the sunshine I felt cold to my bones. And I knew in my innermost being that Richard's body lay here. Moreover I was certain that I was standing right on top of his grave." But would anyone believe her?

TIME LINE

1452

Richard is born, the youngest child of Richard, Duke of York, the House of York's claimant to the throne of England.

1461

After civil war between the Houses of York and Lancaster ("The Wars of the Roses"), Richard's older brother is crowned King Edward IV.

1483

April:
Edward IV dies. His 12-year-old son becomes Edward V. Richard takes custody of Edward and assumes the role of Lord Protector.

June:
Richard and his supporters declare publicly that Edward V is illegitimate.

July:
Richard is crowned King Richard III.

A MILLION TO ONE

Five years later, Langley invited Ashdown-Hill to Edinburgh to give a talk to the local Richard III Society, a group that shared their keen interest in the king. She told him about her instinct; he explained his research. He believed he knew where the Greyfriars church had been located: it must be at the northern end of the parking lot where she had stood. Langley made a decision. With the help of the Richard III Society, she was going to search for the king's grave!

Many people scoffed at the idea that a king was lying forgotten underneath a modern parking lot, but Langley was determined. Like Ashdown-Hill, who guessed

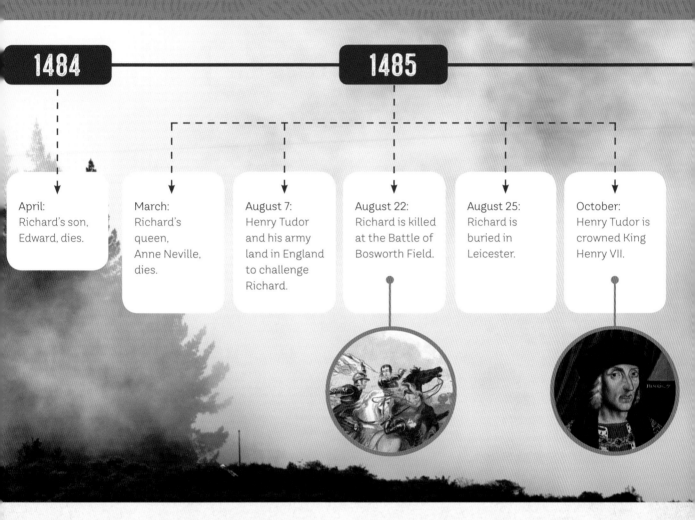

1484

1485

April:
Richard's son,
Edward, dies.

March:
Richard's
queen,
Anne Neville,
dies.

August 7:
Henry Tudor
and his army
land in England
to challenge
Richard.

August 22:
Richard is killed
at the Battle of
Bosworth Field.

August 25:
Richard is
buried in
Leicester.

October:
Henry Tudor is
crowned King
Henry VII.

that clues to the truth might lie in the king's DNA, Langley hoped finding a body would "bring to light the real Richard."

Langley convinced the city council to permit a dig in the parking lot, then met with archaeologist Richard Buckley from the University of Leicester. He was intrigued by the idea of finding the lost Greyfriars church. It might reveal new insights about medieval Leicester and life 500 years ago. They struck a bargain: Buckley's team would search for the church; Langley would keep her fingers crossed that the excavation would also turn up a grave.

Buckley guessed the chances of finding the church were about fifty-fifty. The grave of the king, however, was beyond a long shot. "A million to one," he joked.

TEARING UP THE TARMAC

In August 2012, Buckley's team prepared to break ground. The excavating machine roared into action. Its driver swung the mechanical arm with its clawlike scoop, which began to chew up the tarmac of the first trench. To everyone's disappointment, the first bits of stonework they found turned out to be the remains of a Victorian outhouse.

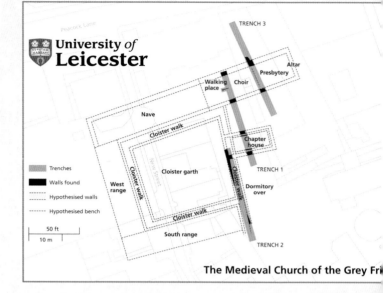

Map of the excavation, with three trenches cut across the parking lot

Matthew Morris, the site director, suddenly raised his hand in the air, and the roar of the excavator stopped. About 1.5 m (5 feet) down, a long bone was visible in the soil. It looked like a leg bone. Using a trowel, Morris gently removed the earth around it. Slowly, a second bone came into view, lying parallel to the first. It looked like two legs, side by side. Could it be part of a skeleton?

Morris reminded Langley not to jump to conclusions. These could be from any century and might belong to anyone. So far they hadn't found a scrap of medieval stonework that might locate the church. In any case, they could not disturb the bones until they had applied for a license to exhume human remains for archaeological purposes.

Medieval reenactors make an appearance at the archaeological dig.

As the dig progressed, bit by bit, evidence of a medieval building came to light—decorated tile and stained glass. Several days into the dig, the team uncovered unmistakable evidence of church walls and graves. It was enough to convince Buckley to apply for a license to exhume the human remains.

BRINGING THE BONES TO LIGHT

Team members prepared to uncover whatever lay alongside the leg bones. They donned forensic suits that covered them from head to foot, to avoid contaminating the bones by shedding their own DNA, and stepped gingerly into the trench. Jo Appleby, an osteoarchaeologist (an archaeologist specializing in human bones), worked with a mattock, an ax-like tool with a broad blade, to chip her way down and look for any more skeletal remains.

It was indeed a human skeleton. The feet were missing—probably cut off when a wall was laid in the 1800s. Other construction had missed the head by millimeters. Possibly this was a friar, buried in the church?

Appleby next uncovered something startling. The skeleton's skull was raised and leaning forward toward the chest, and the spine clearly curved to one side, like a C. Langley was shocked. It couldn't be; she had felt sure that if they found Richard, his spine would be straight, disproving the hostile descriptions. Maybe this wasn't Richard at all. But if it was . . . did that mean the stories about his physical deformities were really true?

The team filmed and photographed the skeleton where it lay. Then each bone was carefully removed and placed in a clear plastic "finds bag." Altogether they fit in a cardboard box. The archaeologists remained cautiously neutral about the identity of the remains. But Langley and Ashdown-Hill felt differently. They had brought a replica of Richard III's royal banner, which they draped over the box before Ashdown-Hill carried it to the waiting van.

TOP & MIDDLE: Archaeologists uncover clues as they excavate the parking lot.

BOTTOM: The skeleton discovered in the first trench

A CASE FOR FORENSIC SCIENCE

The van headed to the University of Leicester. There, a team of experts would analyze the skeleton from different angles. Their approach would be like fitting together the pieces of a puzzle. The bones were treated like a modern forensic case—what would they reveal about the individual, how he died, and possibly *who* he was?

The first step was to conduct a CT scan of the bones (see p. 14). The scientists could now see inside each bone, without cutting anything open. As part of this process, digital images from the CT scan were used with a 3-D printer to create a model of the skeleton. The model skull was so precisely lifelike that even growth rings could be seen!

Meanwhile, the bones were subjected to carbon-14 dating, to get a rough idea of their age (see p. 10). Two samples from rib bones were sent to different labs to cross-check the results.

The outcome was a disappointing setback. It was 95 percent probable that this person had died between 1430 and 1460. But Richard III was killed in 1485. It looked as though the skeleton might be too old to be his.

Then new information added a twist. Other isotopes (different versions of the same chemical element) in the bones revealed details about the person's diet. This man had eaten a lot of seafood. Marine organisms absorb large amounts of carbon-14, so all the seafood he had eaten likely threw off the test. The result was corrected, and now the date of death was 95 percent probable to have been between 1430 and 1530.

Further isotope analysis revealed more clues. Isotopes in teeth formed in childhood and the early teens retain signs of water and food grown in different regions, showing where a person lived while growing up. These matched what was known of Richard's early years—he and his siblings had moved around, often on

NARROWING THE RANGE

Radiocarbon dating cannot pinpoint an exact date; it can only estimate a range of dates along with a percentage of accuracy. Two results are usually given. The first indicates a 68 percent chance that the correct age lies within a span of years; the accuracy increases to 95 percent when the range of years is doubled.

the run from their family's enemies. It was also clear that in the last few years, this person's diet had changed drastically. He'd begun to eat lots of expensive meat, fish, and fowl—a diet of banquets, fit for a king!

RICHARD THE MONSTER?

From the skull, Appleby concluded that this was a man in his late twenties to late thirties (Richard died at 32). A closer look also revealed that he did not have kyphosis, the condition once called "hunchback." The position of the skull, shoved forward onto the chest, had misled her into thinking the back was hunched, but now it was clear this was just because the body had been dropped into a grave that was too short.

Richard III's royal standard with his boar emblem

The upper spine was, however, curved sideways. Its owner had had another condition: scoliosis. The 3-D model of the spine was studied by Piers Mitchell, a scoliosis expert. Scoliosis would not cause a hunch, but the twisting shape of the spine would make the right shoulder slightly higher than the left. This would not have been visible when the person was dressed, and he would have been capable of regular physical activity. The leg bones were normal, so he would not have walked with a limp.

Appleby confirmed that there was no withered arm. Both arms were normal. Whoever he was, he had probably been 1.7 m (5 feet, 8 inches) tall, about average for the Middle Ages.

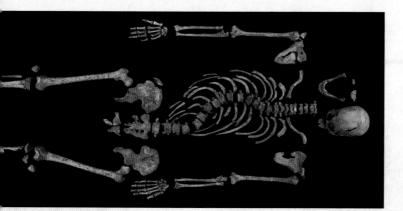

If this *was* Richard III, the bones proved that the stories about his hunchback, limp, and withered arm were deliberate exaggerations and distortions of the truth.

The skeleton of the king? The set of bones are laid out for examination.

FATAL CONTEST

In 2010, the true site of the Battle of Bosworth Field was finally located on the edge of a marsh by archaeologists. Piecing together clues from the battleground with the forensic results from the skeleton, it was at last possible to reconstruct Richard's final minutes.

After Richard's cavalry charge was warded off by Henry's soldiers, armed with pikes, Richard's horse probably lost its footing in the marshy ground, and he was thrown off. Now he was vulnerable in the midst of his enemies, who surrounded him. His helmet was torn away, and his opponents rained blows on his unprotected head. He defended himself vigorously to the end, which came quickly.

THE FINAL BLOW

The next challenge was to determine the cause of death. Appleby was joined by a forensic pathologist and a trauma expert who worked on modern murder cases to identify the source of cut marks in human bone. Robert Woosnam-Savage also joined the examination. As curator of armor and weapons at the Royal Armouries Museum, he was familiar with medieval battle injuries and the weapons that inflicted them. Together they looked at each bone for the slashes of sword wounds or the deeper V-shaped stab marks of daggers.

There was no doubt this man had died a violent death. The skull bones had damage from multiple attacks using different weapons. Two of these blows could have been fatal and were likely made by a halberd (a weapon with an ax blade and spike on top of a wooden shaft). This confirmed one account written shortly after Richard's death: "One of the Welshmen then came after him and struck him dead with a halberd." No battle injuries were found on the body, which must have been well protected by armor. Unusually, the face had been left mostly unharmed. It looked like this victim's attackers had wanted him to remain recognizable after death. Henry Tudor had indeed displayed Richard's body so there would be no doubt that the former king was dead.

FACIAL RECONSTRUCTION:
THE SCIENCE OF RECREATING A HUMAN FACE

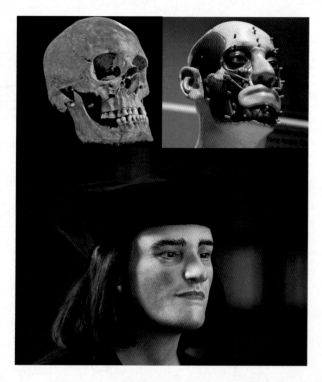

The face of the king: facial reconstruction of Richard III

There are several portraits of Richard III, but these are artists' impressions. Now there was a chance to accurately recreate the face of the king. The science of facial reconstruction, working from a skull outward, has become a proven method of identifying remains in forensic investigations—from murder cases to disaster victims.

A skull is as unique as a face, but we cannot recognize it until the overlying muscles and tissues are added. Digital technology has made the process faster and more accurate. Caroline Wilkinson, an anthropologist and professor of craniofacial identification, worked with high-res photos and 3-D CT scans of the skull. As the image of the skull rotated on her monitor, Wilkinson added eyeballs and tissue. Using a haptic arm—a device that translates the movements of her right arm and hand into on-screen changes—she was able to model the skull like a sculptor working with clay.

A life-size 3-D printout of the head was given to a digital artist, who added hair, skin, and eye color. The finished face took Langley by surprise: "It was the face of a young man who looked as if he were about to speak and to smile. I searched in vain for the tyrant. I can't describe the joy I felt. I was face to face with the real Richard III."

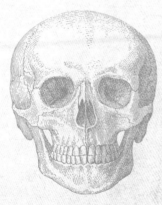

DNA: THE LAST PUZZLE PIECE

A royal tomb for Richard III in Leicester Cathedral

It was time to proceed with a DNA comparison to a living descendant of Richard's sister. Ibsen's son Michael lived in London, where he worked as a cabinetmaker, and he had agreed to give a live DNA sample, taken at the parking-lot dig itself. The DNA evidence would be the most essential piece to clinch the identification.

Ancient DNA is delicate. Teeth are often the best-preserved parts of a skeleton, and the femur is thick, so samples were taken from each of these. If both samples yielded the same results, it would help to rule out the possibility that the DNA had been contaminated. The DNA sequencing was carried out by two labs that specialized in ancient DNA to cross-check the results.

Ibsen's DNA was then compared to the skeleton's DNA sequence produced by both labs. Both yielded the same result: a perfect match! All the evidence was next subjected to a statistical analysis. The probability that the skeleton belonged to Richard III lay between 99.9994 and 99.9999 percent.

The team of archaeologists and scientists made their announcement to the world at a press conference. After the experts went through the evidence, Buckley declared that "beyond reasonable doubt, the individual exhumed at Greyfriars in September 2012 is indeed Richard III, the last Plantagenet king of England."

THE RETURN OF THE KING

In 2015, King Richard III was reinterred in Leicester Cathedral, in a coffin made by his seventeenth-generation nephew Michael Ibsen. Langley was satisfied that one of her crucial goals had been accomplished: an honorable reburial for Richard in the royal tomb that Henry VII had denied him.

A statue honoring
Richard III in Leicester

Langley's far-fetched hunch had paid off. The archaeologists pointed out that this was an amazing find, not just because Richard was a king, but because finding a named individual 500 years old, along with the opportunity to analyze the remains, is "extraordinarily rare." By applying analysis from every relevant stream of knowledge—genetics, medicine, forensics, genealogy, history, and archaeology—the researchers were able to look in incredible detail at the life of a king from the vanished Middle Ages. His life and times—how and where he grew up, what he ate and drank, and the wounds that killed him—were all brought to light.

What we thought we knew . . . and what we know now

So, was Richard a good king whose reign was cut short by treason or a deposed tyrant? The evidence of the bones helped to strike a balance between the two extremes: by confirming what grains of truth lay in the confusion of accounts, a reputation was restored and a caricature turned back into a recognizable human being.

Perhaps the last king of England's Middle Ages was a man of his stormy times, a capable person in whom ambition and a sense of duty coexisted. The truths about his character and his intentions are still left for historians to puzzle over.

The search for King Richard III has taught us that in looking for the truth about a person, science can be applied not just to a skeleton but to history as well. What history has long told us about Richard was held up to the same kind of scientific test as the bones. Legend and fact were separated—the king was not a monster, his body was never thrown in the river, and his coffin was not turned into a horse trough. If these parts of the historical record were untrue, what else might be? The discovery of the lost king is a powerful reminder to view historical "facts" with an open and objective mind.

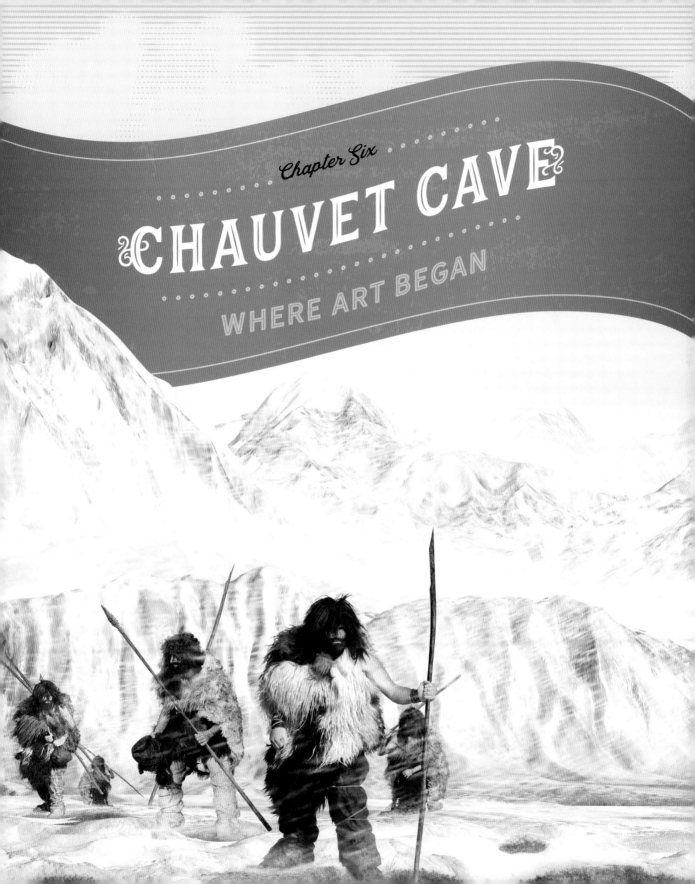

Chapter Six

CHAUVET CAVE

WHERE ART BEGAN

THE AIR IS DRY AND COLD, but the men walking along the foot of the cliffs are warm in their coats and boots of reindeer skin and fur. Higher up in the mountains, everything is covered with a thick layer of glacial ice, but here, there are prairies of low-growing trees and thin pine forests.

To survive, these men follow the huge herds of reindeer, horse, and bison that run across the grassy expanses. These they hunt with long spears—they sometimes even take down the woolly mammoth. At night, they sleep in open-air camps or under the rocky cliffsides, where they warm themselves around a fire and take turns watching for predators: cave bears, cave lions, and the woolly rhinoceros.

Not far from their campfire, two cliffs connect over the fast-flowing river with a soaring arch of limestone. It is a landmark they all know well. Near it, an opening in the cliffside leads into darkness. The people who venture inside find the passage opens into a lofty chamber with limestone walls.

They bring pine torches with them, casting a flickering glow in the immense darkness. They build fires on the cave floor and burn pine to make pigment from charcoal. One of the men covers his palm with red ocher and presses it against the cool limestone wall of the cave, leaving his unique mark. It will remain for millennia.

An artist imagines a gathering of prehistoric humans.

Who they were, what they were doing, and why will become mysteries lost in unimaginable stretches of time, but they will leave clues—in red ocher and charcoal. When those clues are rediscovered, and studied with modern technology, they will entirely change our understanding of the evolution of humans as artists. Startling evidence of genius at the very dawn of human art will shed light on our beginnings as intelligent, creative—and possibly spiritual—beings.

SEARCHING FOR THE FIRST ARTISTS

Throughout the world, our distant ancestors left their imprint with painted images on cave walls. In Europe, Spain, and France, there have been discovery sites of especially spectacular prehistoric cave art.

ANCIENT ANCESTORS

During the Paleolithic Period (or Old Stone Age), humans and their extinct ancestors were hunter-gatherers who relied on stone tools chipped into shape by using one stone like a hammer to strike another. This stage of human development lasted from about 2.5 million years ago to the end of the last ice age, about 9600 BCE.

Based on these discoveries, experts devised a time line of progress in human art. The oldest known cave images were crude, simple line drawings—probably not intended to look like anything realistic. Over the course of many thousands of years, the artists' clumsy attempts slowly evolved and became more sophisticated, until finally they mastered the accurate depictions of animals— a milestone in human artistry. This time line was widely accepted.

And then came a truly astonishing discovery. In 1940, French archaeologist Henri Breuil was summoned to the region of Lascaux in the south of France. A group of boys had discovered a cave with amazingly realistic images on its walls— a colorful gallery of bulls, aurochs, and other animals. Breuil was so astounded that he dubbed the cave "the Sistine Chapel of Prehistory." Here, humans had reached a height of artistry not yet seen in prehistoric painting. For decades, the Lascaux cave paintings—dated at 17,000 years old—were thought to be the first sophisticated artworks of the prehistoric era: this, people said, was where art had truly begun.

A GAP IN THE CLIFFSIDE:
AND A STUNNING DISCOVERY

France's Ardèche River runs through gorges flanked by steep limestone cliffs. At the famous Pont d'Arc, the limestone spans the river in a striking natural stone arch.

On a clear, cold Sunday in December 1994, three friends were roaming the cliff-side trails, pursuing their favorite hobby: exploring caves, or spelunking. Leading the way was Jean-Marie Chauvet, a local park ranger. With him were Éliette Brunel Deschamps and Christian Hillaire. They spent the day threading the narrow ledges on the sides of the cliffs and entering every opening they found.

Beyond the straggly trees that clung to the rock face, they spotted a small opening in the white cliff above. It was narrow, barely big enough for them to squeeze through one by one. Inside, they found themselves in a small, dry chamber. The floor sloped downward, and the three friends followed it until they hit a rubble-filled dead end.

The famous natural stone arch at Pont d'Arc, France

Chauvet felt a draft coming through the stones blocking their way. This was a sign that there might be a cavern hidden behind the blockage. The draft felt strong enough to investigate. They took turns pulling away the stones so they could inch forward.

At last, Brunel Deschamps fit her head and shoulders through the narrow opening. With her headlamp, she could see a floor far below, perhaps 10 m (33 feet) down. There was a cavern! Excited, they shouted and listened for the echo—but their voices seemed to carry on endlessly.

A VAST AND SPARKLING SPACE

The three friends returned with a cable ladder and, squeezing through the gap, climbed down one by one. Chauvet touched the bottom first.

The silence engulfing him was total. Looking around, he saw that the chamber was even higher and vaster than he had imagined. Everything his helmet light touched upon was white and sparkling. Columns of white calcite in fantastic shapes sprung from the floor like giant cacti or hung from the lofty ceiling in waves like draperies. He knew these had taken many thousands of years to form. It was so beautiful that no one spoke.

Moving in single file, they each traced the footsteps of the person ahead so as not to damage the white calcite floor. Their eyes were drawn to an opening on their

A replica of Lascaux Cave and its artworks created for visitors now that the original cave is closed to protect it

TOP: A cave explorer comes across huge icicle-like stalactites.

BOTTOM: Hanging from the cave's roof, stalactites are mineral deposits formed over thousands of years from slowly dripping water.

left. It led to a second chamber—in all their exploring, they had never been inside a cave this huge! On the floor, Chauvet spotted bear skulls and teeth scattered everywhere.

Suddenly, Brunel Deschamps broke the silence. "They were here!" she cried out.

The beam of her light struck a pendant of rock hanging from the ceiling. Red lines formed a shape on it—unmistakably the outline of a mammoth.

Not only bears had been here but prehistoric humans, too! Chauvet's heart pounded as he swung his headlamp along the walls. In the middle of a white expanse, a huge red bear came into sight. Now they all knew they had stumbled onto something extraordinary.

STEPPING BACK IN TIME

They retraced their steps, examining the walls more carefully this time. A few paces back was the image of a huge rhinoceros, then a bear—and three lions! A long mural ran down another wall: large red dots formed an animal shape. And then, red handprints—the human touch of the artist.

Chauvet realized that they must be the first people to walk there in thousands of years. The cave was pristine; the paintings stood out as vividly as if they had just been completed. He was gripped by a bizarre feeling: "Everything was so beautiful, so fresh . . . Time was abolished . . . Suddenly we felt like intruders . . . We thought we could feel their presence; we were disturbing them."

That night, they returned with more powerful flashlights. Their beams lit up a wall at the far end of the chamber, revealing a sight that left everyone breathless. Covering more than 10 m (33 feet) was a magnificent scene in black charcoal. Their lights danced over a herd of running horses, their heads lifelike with wide eyes and open muzzles. Nearby, two rhinos faced each other, locking horns in a fight. A bison with many legs seemed to depict running. The animals appeared to ripple over the wall's contours, creating an uncanny effect of depth and movement.

GOING PUBLIC

Chauvet knew that archaeologists and scientists would be keen to see their amazing discovery for themselves. On December 28, he contacted the authorities.

Jean Clottes, a well-known archaeologist and prehistoric art expert, set out the same day with two other archaeologists to join the original discoverers. Brunel Deschamps had brought champagne, expecting to celebrate. Clottes, on the other hand, doubted their story and expected to find a hoax. But the expert was soon convinced. The film of ancient calcite covering the drawings had taken many thousands of years to grow and was formed long after the paintings were done. It was impossible that these were modern forgeries.

More experts arrived to authenticate the cave art. All were grateful to the group of discoverers who had been so careful to touch nothing and limit the damage done by their footsteps to a single track.

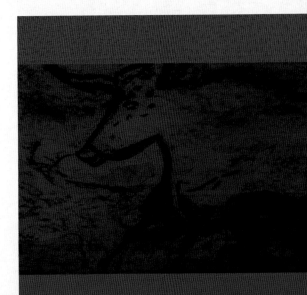

SPOTTING A FAKE

Hoaxes and fakes in Paleolithic art are rare, but they have happened. It took a great deal of study to discover that the "prehistoric" art found in the cave of Zubialde, Spain, was a forgery. It had been carefully done with natural pigments and imitated animals already seen in other cave art. But in recent years, it had been discovered that charcoal was commonly used in these paintings, and in Zubialde, charcoal was suspiciously absent. And two more obvious clues gave the forgery away. The insect pigment used in the paintings could not possibly have lasted thousands of years. And, worse, close inspection revealed remnants of synthetic sponge!

HOW OLD *IS* IT?
USING TECHNOLOGY TO DATE THE ART

Inspection under a magnifying glass showed that the painted lines contained tiny gaps caused by erosion. And the engraved lines were full of micro-crystallizations formed over thousands of years.

Clearly the cave art was thousands of years old—but how old was it exactly? Clottes was perplexed by the "powerful originality" of the art; it was like nothing he had ever seen. Still, all the clues and comparisons to other known cave art led the experts to estimate that they were painted between 17,000 and 21,000 years ago, roughly the same time as the Lascaux paintings.

The next step was to use radiocarbon dating on samples of organic material (see p. 10). While the red paintings were made with iron oxide, the charcoal used to make the black paintings had come from burning the wood of a tree, and so its carbon-14 decay could be tested. Three tiny samples of charcoal were taken from paintings of two rhinos and a bison and sent to a lab.

Visitors view a replica of Chauvet Cave built by the French government. The original cave is too fragile to be open to the public.

The results came as a complete shock. The three samples from the paintings were all produced in the same period—around 31,000 years ago. No one had expected this. These paintings were made more than 10,000 years *before* the paintings in the Lascaux caves. More charcoal samples from the images were gathered—and these were *even older!* Most of the paintings in Chauvet Cave were done between 33,500 and 37,000 years ago.

The news sent a shockwave through the worlds of art and archaeology alike. The art of Chauvet Cave was twice as old as the art of Lascaux, but it was *more* masterly and sophisticated.

> **"THESE NEW DATES OVERTURN OUR CONCEPTIONS ... ABOUT THE BEGINNINGS OF ART."**
> —Jean Clottes

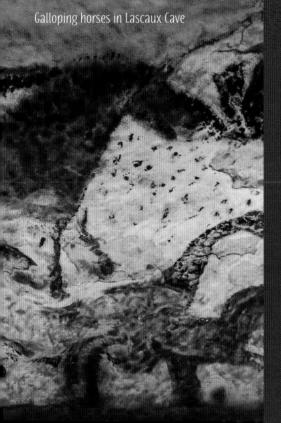

Galloping horses in Lascaux Cave

CLUES IN THE PIGMENT

Scientific analysis of prehistoric art has come a long way, thanks to innovations in technology.

- Scanning electron microscope (SEM): This instrument scans the surface of an object with a narrow beam of electrons. The beam causes electrons to scatter back from the object. This allows scientists to produce a detailed image of the object and to reproduce its chemical structure.
- X-ray technologies: These are also used to reveal the structure of objects and what chemical elements they are made of.
- Accelerator mass spectrometry (AMS): This test can count the number of carbon-14 atoms in a tiny speck of pigment. The sample needed is so small that cave art can be dated without harming the painting. It can accurately date objects as old as 55,000 years.

UNEXPECTED MASTERPIECES

Chauvet and his friends had stumbled upon the oldest-known realistic paintings in the world. And nothing about them fit into what experts believed about the evolution of art.

Most cave art shows the animals that Ice Age humans hunted: horses, reindeer, bison, and the now-extinct aurochs. But in Chauvet Cave, fierce and dangerous animals dominate the walls—the ones humans feared rather than hunted. Rhinos, lions, and mammoths are rare in Paleolithic art, but in Chauvet, they appear the most often among the more than 400 painted animals. Why did the artists make this choice? What did painting these fearsome beasts mean to them?

And these are sophisticated works of art, not the simple line drawings or symbols that archaeologists would have expected. The artists of Chauvet created lifelike, realistic animals in convincing detail. Each scene is full of movement and energy.

Caverne du Pont d'Arc, an exact replica of Chauvet Cave, was built nearby for visitors.

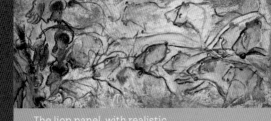

The lion panel, with realistic, overlapping profiles

IMITATING LIFE

To achieve such lifelike realism, the artists of Chauvet used a number of techniques.

- **Perspective:** The painted animals overlap, creating an impression of depth and the look of a big herd. Animals were drawn where the wall surface bulges or curves, creating a 3-D effect.

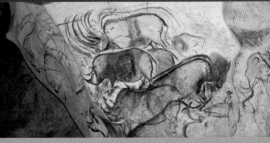

A group of rhinos—one has many horns to depict motion

- **Shading:** Charcoal was used to contour the animals' bodies—it was spread with a tool or the palm to get gradations from light to dark, an extremely rare technique in cave art.

- **Illusion of motion:** The animals fight or chase one another; herds stampede. One bison is painted with many legs to convey the idea of running.

The panel of horses with its complex shading and composition

- **Scraping:** This method was used to prep the walls, making the images stand out against a smoother, whiter background.

- **Stump-drawing:** In this technique, particles of charcoal or ocher were crushed and spread to blend colors together or to create intermediate shades.

A horse engraved with a finger on a film of clay, now hardened.

All these techniques were combined in one of the cave's most stunning masterpieces—the panel of the horses that awed Chauvet and his friends.

A profile of the extinct cave bear

TIME LINE

c. 40,000 YEARS AGO

↓

Upper Paleolithic Period begins:
- Stone tools become more complex. Bone, ivory, and antler are also used in toolmaking.
- Humans create small sculptured pieces of art: clay figurines, carved bone and ivory, and portable stone statuettes.

c. 37 000–33,500 YEARS AGO

↓

Human activity and painting in Chauvet Cave.

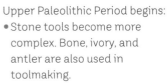

c. 35,000 YEARS AGO

↓

Evidence of musical instruments carved from bone or ivory.

MYSTERY ARTISTS:
WHO WERE THEY, AND WHY DID THEY PAINT?

Although it's clear that not everything was painted at the same time or by the same person (because of differences in skill and style), a large number of the black paintings are so similar, their lines drawn so confidently, that art experts are sure they are the work of a single master artist. Other clues can be found in the red handprints and negative hand stencils made by placing the hand on the wall and blowing pigment over it. In these, human beings left their individual marks. One of the artists who left his handprint had a crooked little finger, and so it's possible to trace

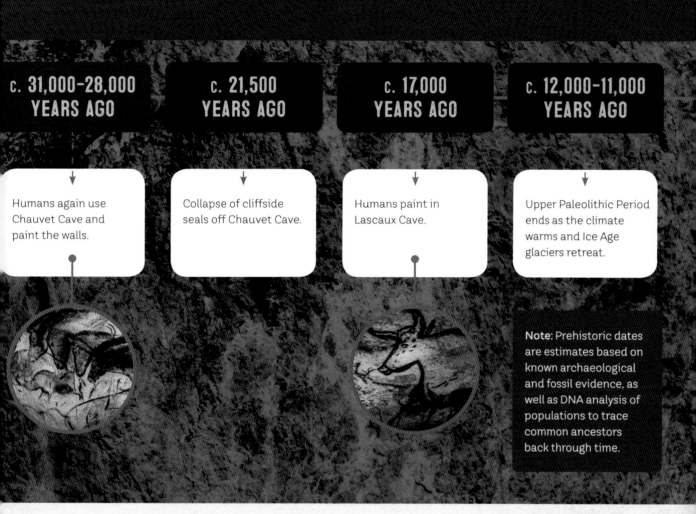

c. 31,000–28,000 YEARS AGO	c. 21,500 YEARS AGO	c. 17,000 YEARS AGO	c. 12,000–11,000 YEARS AGO
Humans again use Chauvet Cave and paint the walls.	Collapse of cliffside seals off Chauvet Cave.	Humans paint in Lascaux Cave.	Upper Paleolithic Period ends as the climate warms and Ice Age glaciers retreat.

Note: Prehistoric dates are estimates based on known archaeological and fossil evidence, as well as DNA analysis of populations to trace common ancestors back through time.

his "signature" throughout the cave. Analysis of the relative lengths of the fingers has led some experts to conclude that both male and female prints are present. If so, this challenges a long-standing belief that these early artists were male, painting the animals they hunted.

But why did they paint? A clue may lie in the fact that very few images are near the original cave entrance, where sunlight would have made it easier to paint and see the art. Instead, the artists painted deep within the

NO PEOPLE

Interestingly, among all the paintings, there are almost no depictions of humans. One exception is the lower body of a woman connected to a bison head. Here, realism has been deliberately abandoned—it looks more like pure imagination!

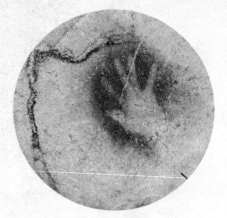

A hand stencil in Chauvet Cave

caverns, working in darkness with only the glow of their torches. Besides total darkness, there is complete silence in the cave. It is likely that the artists who used these caves over 35,000 years ago chose the site for these very reasons.

One theory that many experts support is that the purpose of the art was all about the act of painting itself. Maybe the painting in Chauvet Cave was a spiritual act linked to shamanism, a religion widespread among hunter-gatherers throughout the ages. For the people of Chauvet Cave, the human world, the animal world, and the spirit world would all have been interconnected. Certain people, the shamans, could move between the worlds by entering a trance-like state. Descending into the mysterious, dark, and silent world of the caves could be one way to do that. Painting and engraving the rocks where spirits lived might have been a way to contact them and win their goodwill and perhaps even some of their power.

MIDDLE & BOTTOM: Displays at the Chauvet Cave replica recreate life in the Paleolithic Period.

LIFE IN THE ICE AGE:
CHAUVET'S CLUES

Thanks to its unspoiled condition, Chauvet Cave
has preserved a vivid picture of life so many
millennia ago. Claw marks, bones, and sleep-
ing dugouts show that cave bears (now extinct)
hibernated there as early as 48,500 years ago.
Sensibly, humans painted in the cave only after
the bears had abandoned it. After all, the cave
bear was a 400 kg (880-pound) carnivore!

People arrived in the caves around 36,500
years ago. Human footprints are preserved in
the floor—including a child's. But they did not
live in the caves. There are no human bones,
signs of hearths, or leftover animal bones from
their food.

EXTINCT ANIMALS
Details of the art in
Chauvet Cave tell us about extinct
animals. It is impossible to tell
from fossil remains whether the
male cave lion of the Ice Age had
a mane like today's African lions.
From the paintings at Chauvet,
it is clear he did not!

Neanderthals, now extinct, were related
to modern humans. Early in the Upper
Paleolithic Period, they lived at the
same time as humans in Europe.

It is most likely that the decorated chambers were used for ceremonies—probably shamanistic. People built fires to light their work and to make charcoal for the art. Heaps of charcoal remain on the floors. They carried torches, made from Scotch pine, whose traces of wiping are still on the walls. When a torch burns down to charcoal, it can be revived by rubbing it against stone, and the wipes are the traces left behind. Some torch wipes are on top of the calcite over the paintings, showing that people came to the cave long after the paintings were done.

The extinct cave lion, as revealed in the art of Chauvet

Cave bears, now extinct, once lived in Chauvet Cave.

During the Ice Age, the original entrance to the cave was not where Chauvet and his friends crawled through. It was larger and could be seen from the valley. Geologists determined that the cliffside fell 21,500 years ago in a rockslide that closed off the cave to humans and animals. The caverns were sealed, like a time capsule—the reason why everything inside remained in such perfect condition.

What we thought we knew . . . and what we know now

The amazing art of Chauvet Cave proved that humans were ambitious artists tens of thousands of years earlier than anyone ever imagined. And these early humans were already self-aware, abstract thinkers able to express their ideas with sophisticated techniques. We can guess, too, that the paintings had a ritual role, suggesting that our ancient ancestors had spiritual beliefs as well.

Artistic excellence also varied from region to region, as well as from time to time. It's possible there are even older examples that have not yet been found. For instance, hand stencils and depictions of animals later discovered on cave walls in Indonesia were found to be at least as old as, if not older than, the cave art of Chauvet. Still, no other discovery has yet rivaled the excellence and ambition of the masterpieces at Chauvet Cave.

Archaeologist Paul G. Bahn says the discoveries at Chauvet Cave teach us that our current knowledge is still incomplete and likely to change. But this is true, he adds, of all archaeology, an ongoing search "where a single find—be it a hominid bone, the Iceman, or a new cave—can cause all the textbooks to be rewritten."

MAIN SOURCES

DETECTIVES OF THE PAST

National Geographic. "Space Archaeology 101: The Next Frontier of Exploration."
National Geographic: Video. Web.

ÖTZI THE ICEMAN

Dickson, James H., et al. "The Iceman reconsidered." *Scientific American*, January 2005. Web.

Fagan, Brian M., editor. *Eyewitness to Discovery: First-Person Accounts of More Than Fifty of the World's Greatest Archaeological Discoveries*. Oxford: Oxford University Press, 1996.

Hall, Stephen S. "Unfrozen." *National Geographic*, November 2011. Web.

"Neolithic Period." *Encyclopaedia Britannica*. Web.

"Ötzi the Iceman." *South Tyrol Museum of Archaeology*. Web.

DEADLY KNOWLEDGE

Contenta, Sandro. "England's Poison Garden an ode to death by greenery." *The Toronto Star*, 12 February 2017. Web.

d'Errico, F., et al. "Early evidence of San material culture represented by organic artifacts from Border Cave, South Africa." *Proceedings of the National Academy of Sciences of the United States of America*, 109.33, 14 August 2012. Web.

Kentish, Franky. "The Poison Garden plants once used as prehistoric weaponry." *The Telegraph*, 20 March 2015. Web.

"Later Stone Age got earlier start in South Africa than thought, says CU researcher." *CU Boulder Today*. University of Colorado Boulder, 30 July 2012. Web.

Pappas, Stephanie. "Oldest poison pushes back ancient civilization 20,000 years." *Live Science*, 30 July 2012. Web.

"Poisons, plants and Palaeolithic hunters." *Research at Cambridge*. University of Cambridge, 21 March 2015. Web.

Villa, Paola et al. "Border Cave and the beginning of the Later Stone Age in South Africa." *Proceedings of the National Academy of Sciences of the United States of America*, 109.33, 14 August 2012. Web.

UNDER THE JUNGLE

Associated Press. "Laser technology reveals lost city around Angkor Wat." *The Guardian*, 18 June 2013. Web.

Bahn, Paul. *Archaeology: A Very Short Introduction*. Oxford: Oxford University Press, 2012.

Bryner, Jeanna. "'Lost' medieval city discovered beneath Cambodian jungle." *Live Science*, 18 June 2013. Web.

Daguan, Zhou. *A Record of Cambodia: The Land and Its People*. Translated by Peter Harris. 2007. Chiang Mai, Thailand: Silkworm Books, 2013.

Dunston, Lara. "Revealed: Cambodia's vast medieval cities hidden beneath the jungle." *The Guardian*, 11 June 2016. Web.

Evans, Damian. "Airborne laser scanning as a method for exploring long-term socio-ecological dynamics in Cambodia," *Journal of Archaeological Science*, vol. 74, October 2016. Web.

Evans, Damian. "Uncovering the real Angkor: Early civilisations mapped using cutting-edge technology." Royal Geographical Society, 13 June 2016, London. Lecture. Web.

Evans, Damian, et al. "Uncovering archaeological landscapes at Angkor using lidar." *Proceedings of the National Academy of Sciences of the United States of America*, 110.31, 30 July 2013. Web.

LOST SHIPS OF THE ARCTIC

"The Franklin Expedition." *Parks Canada*. Web.

Geiger, John, and Alanna Mitchell. *Franklin's Lost Ship: The Historic Discovery of HMS Erebus*. Toronto: HarperCollins Publishers Ltd., 2015.

Watson, Paul. *Ice Ghosts: The Epic Hunt for the Lost Franklin Expedition*. Toronto: McClelland & Stewart, 2017.

Watson, Paul. "Ship found in Arctic 168 years after doomed Northwest Passage attempt." *The Guardian*, 12 September 2016. Web.

Woodman, David C. *Unravelling the Franklin Mystery: Inuit Testimony*, Second Edition. Montreal: McGill-Queen's University Press, 2015.

HIDDEN MAJESTY

Ashdown-Hill, John. *The Last Days of Richard III and the Fate of his DNA*, Revised Edition. Stroud, UK: The History Press, 2013.

Carson, A.J., editor. *Finding Richard III: The Official Account of Research by the Retrieval and Reburial Project*. Horstead, UK: Imprimus Imprimatur, 2014.

Dockray, Keith, and Peter Hammond. *Richard III: From Contemporary Chronicles, Letters & Records*. Oxford: Fonthill Media Ltd., 2013.

Greyfriars Research Team, et al. *The Bones of a King: Richard III Rediscovered*. Oxford: John Wiley & Sons, 2015.

Kennedy, Maev. "Archaeologists pinpoint long-disputed site of Battle of Bosworth." *The Guardian*, 19 February 2010. Web.

Langley, Philippa, and Michael Jones. *The King's Grave: The Discovery of Richard III's Lost Burial Place and the Clues It Holds*. New York: St. Martin's Press, 2013.

CHAUVET CAVE

Bahn, Paul G. *Cave Art*, Revised Edition. London: Frances Lincoln, 2012.

"Cave of Forgotten Dreams." Directed by Werner Herzog. IFC Films, 2011.

Chauvet, Jean-Marie, et al. *Dawn of Art: the Chauvet Cave: The Oldest Known Paintings in the World*. Translated by Paul G. Bahn. London: Thames and Hudson Ltd., 1996.

"The Chauvet-Pont d'Arc Cave, Ardèche." *Grands sites archéologiques*. Ministry of Culture and Communication. Web.

Clottes, Jean. *Cave Art*. London: Phaidon Press Ltd., 2008.

Clottes, Jean. "Chauvet-Pont d'Arc," *Encyclopaedia Britannica*, 4 August, 2015. Web.

David, Bruno. *Cave Art*. New York: Thames & Hudson Ltd., 2017.

Zorich, Zach. "New dates for the oldest cave paintings." *Archaeology Magazine*. Archaeological Institute of America, 13 June 2016. Web.

FURTHER READING

ARCHAEOLOGY

Orna-Ornstein, John. *Archaeology: Discovering the Past*. New York: Oxford University Press, 2002.

Moloney, Norah. *The Young Oxford Book of Archaeology*. Oxford: Oxford University Press, 2000.

Niver, Heather Moore, editor. *Archaeology: Excavating Our Past*. New York: Britannica Educational Publishing, 2015.

ÖTZI THE ICEMAN

Lanser, Amanda. *Ötzi the Iceman*. Minneapolis, Abdo Publishing, 2015.

Meyer, Susan. *The Neolithic Revolution*. The First Humans and Early Civilizations. New York: Rosen Young Adult, 2017.

Walker, Richard. *Genes & DNA*. Boston: Kingfisher, 2003.

DEADLY KNOWLEDGE

Dauncey, Elizabeth A., and Sonny Larsson. *Plants that Kill: A Natural History of the World's Most Poisonous Plants*. Princeton: Princeton University Press, 2018.

Wilkinson, Philip, editor. *Early Humans*. DK Eyewitness Books. New York: DK, 2005.

UNDER THE JUNGLE

Behnke, Alison. *Angkor Wat*. Unearthing Ancient Worlds. Minneapolis: Twenty-First Century Books, 2009.

Goldberg, Jan. *Earth Imaging Satellites*. New York: Rosen Publishing Group, 2003.

LOST SHIPS OF THE ARCTIC

Berton, Pierre. *Exploring the Frozen North*. Calgary: Fifth House, 2006.

Hutchinson, Gillian. *Sir John Franklin's Erebus and Terror Expedition: Lost and Found*. London: Adlard Coles Nautical, 2017.

HIDDEN MAJESTY

Wheatley, Abigail, et al. *The Middle Ages*. Usborne History of Britain. London: Usborne, 2008.

Morris, Matthew, and Richard Buckley. *Richard III: The King Under the Car Park*. Leicester: University of Leicester School of Archaeology and Ancient History, 2013.

Throp, Claire. *The Split History of the Wars of the Roses*. Oxford: Raintree, 2016.

CHAUVET CAVE

Brooke, Beatrice D., and Roberto Carvalho de Magalhaes. *Art and Culture of the Prehistoric World*. New York: Rosen Publishing Group, 2010.

Johanson, Paula. *The Paleolithic Revolution*. The First Humans and Early Civilizations. New York: Rosen Young Adult, 2017.

Lauber, Patricia. *Painters of the Caves*. Washington, D.C.: National Geographic Society, 1998.

INDEX

IMAGE CREDITS

Cover images: (bones) Audrey Shtecinjo / Stocksy.com; (bear skull) Audrey Snider-Bell / Shutterstock; (sword) Artur Balytski / Shutterstock; (crown) bioraven / Shutterstock.

Background images: (bones) Audrey Shtecinjo / Stocksy.com; (bear skull) Audrey Snider-Bell / Shutterstock; (sword) Artur Balytski / Shutterstock; (crown) bioraven / Shutterstock.

Design elements: (grunge medallion) Larysa Ray / Shutterstock; (paper) PremiumVector / Shutterstock; (paperclips, folded paper) Hilch / Shutterstock; (magnifying glass) mrgao / iStockphoto.com; (skull) Hein Nouwens / Shutterstock; (sticky note) Lyudmyla Kharlamova / Shutterstock; (archaeology tools) Noch / Shutterstock; (crown) bioraven / Shutterstock; (notepaper) Picsfive /Shutterstock; (medieval symbols) Artur Balytski / Shutterstock.

Frontispiece: Audrey Shtecinjo / Stocksy.com

All maps by Bambi Edlund; Background image by jumpingjack / Shutterstock.

4 Masarik / Shutterstock; **5** Microgen / Shutterstock.

Chapter 1: 7 (Illustration of one of the theories about the death of Ötzi the Iceman) SMETEK / Science Photo Library; **8** Wikimedia Commons contributors, "File:Similaun 7.jpg," Wikimedia Commons, the free media repository; **9** Photo by Paul Hanny / Gamma-Rapho via Getty Images; **10** © South Tyrol Museum of Archaeology / Paul Hanny; **11** (top) World History Archive / Alamy Stock Photo; **11** (bottom) © Kenneth Garrett; **12** (top) imageBROKER / Alamy Stock Photo; (centre) © Kenneth Garrett; (bottom) prapann / Shutterstock; (mountain) Macgork / Shutterstock; **13** David Lyons / Alamy Stock Photo; **14–15** (timeline background) Colin Rex / Unsplash; (timeline images from left to right) Photo by Paul Hanny / Gamma-Rapho via Getty Images; Ant_art / Shutterstock; Roberto La Rosa / Shutterstock; **15** (skull) Hein Nouwens / Shutterstock; **16** (arrow) VectorPlotnikoff / Shutterstock; (bottom) © South Tyrol Museum of Archaeology / Eurac / Samadelli / Staschitz; **17** © South Tyrol Museum of Archaeology / Augustin Ochsenreiter; **18** © South Tyrol Museum of Archaeology / FlipFlop Collective; **20** isak55/ Shutterstock; **21** (girl) CGN089 / Shutterstock.

Chapter 2: 23 (San family hunting in the Kalahari Desert of southern Africa) franco lucato / Shutterstock; **24** 2630ben / Shutterstock; **25** (top) pterwort / Shutterstock; (bottom) Androstachys / Wikimedia; **26** (top) franco lucato / Shutterstock; (skull) The Natural History Museum / Alamy Stock Photo; (sticks) © Francesco d'Errico; **27** (top) © Francesco d'Errico; (bottom) Jelena Aloskina / Shutterstock; **28** (timeline background) Joe McDaniel / Unsplash; **28–29** (timeline images from left to right) 2630ben / Shutterstock; © Francesco d'Errico; Ricardo de Paula Ferreira / Shutterstock; **29** (sign) R Scapinello /Shutterstock; **29** (belladonna illustration) Morphart Creation / Shutterstock; **30** (plant illustration) Morphart Creation / Shutterstock; (bottom) Izel Photography / Alamy Stock Photo / All Canada Photos; **31** (left to right) Martin Fowler /Shutterstock; Nick Pecker / Shutterstock; R Scapinello /Shutterstock; **32** (top) Stuart Walker / Alamy Stock Photo; (bottom) curved-light / Alamy Stock Photo; **33** (plant illustration) Hein Nouwens / Shutterstock; (boy) espies / Shutterstock.

Chapter 3: 35 (An artist's depiction of the building of Angkor Wat) imageBROKER / Alamy Stock Photo; **36** Illustration from Henri Mouhot, *Voyage dans les royaumes de Siam, de Cambodge, de Laos et autres parties centrales de l'Indochine* (published 1863, 1864); **37** Morphart Creation / Shutterstock; **38** David Wall / Alamy Stock Photo / All Canada Photos; **39** (top) De Visu / Shutterstock;

(bottom) Perfect Lazybones / Shutterstock; **40** The Cambodian Archaeological Lidar Initiative; **41** Till Sonnemann / ETH Zurich; **42** Courtesy image of The Cambodian Archaeological Lidar Initiative; **43** Gail Palethorpe / Shutterstock; **44** World History Archive / Alamy Stock Photo / All Canada Photos; **45** (top) Matyas Rehak / Shutterstock; (bottom) Bussakorn Ewesakul / Shutterstock; **46–47** (timeline background) Spencer Watson / Unsplash; (timeline images from left to right) David Wall / Alamy Stock Photo / All Canada Photos; SantiPhotoSS / Shutterstock; DeltaOFF / Shutterstock; (monkey) Davdeka / Shutterstock; **48–49** (background) SaveJungle / Shutterstock; **48** David Wall / Alamy Stock Photo / All Canada Photos; **49** (girl) Jfunk / Shutterstock.

Chapter 4: 51 (Nineteenth-century painting of the Franklin expedition) INTERFOTO / Alamy Stock Photo / All Canada Photos; **52** Library and Archives Canada, Acc. No. 1955-102-53; **53** (top) Library and Archives Canada, Peter Winkworth Collection of Canadiana, R9666-3035; (bottom) Science History Images / Alamy Stock Photo; **54** (top) ThomasLENNE / Shutterstock; (bottom) Library and Archives Canada, Acc. No. 1981-70-15 Source: Mr. J. Coles, Ottawa, Ontario; **55** (top) Marzolino / Shutterstock; (bottom) North Wind Picture Archives / Alamy Stock Photo; **56** Marzolino / Shutterstock; **57** Universal Images Group North America LLC / Alamy Stock Photo / All Canada Photos; **58–59** (timeline background) asoggetti / Unsplash; (timeline images from left to right) Wildnerdpix / Shutterstock; Science History Images / Alamy Stock Photo; INTERFOTO / Alamy Stock Photo / All Canada Photos; **58** (bottom) Parks Canada; **61** National Snow and Ice Data Center, courtesy Ted Scambos and Rob Bauer; **62–66** Parks Canada; **67** 2d Alan King / Alamy Stock Photo / All Canada Photos; **68** Parks Canada; **69** (boy) sashahaltam / Shutterstock.

Chapter 5: 71 (Richard III at the Battle of Bosworth Field) duncan1890 / iStockphoto; **72** From Doyle, James William Edmund (1864), "Richard III" in A Chronicle of England: B.C. 55–A.D. 1485, London: Longman, Green, Longman, Roberts & Green; **73** From *The National Portrait Gallery History of the Kings and Queens of England* by David Williamson; **74** Geraint Lewis / Alamy Stock Photo / All Canada Photos; **76** Georgios Kollidas / Shutterstock; **77** (bones) D.R.3D / Shutterstock; **78–79** (timeline background) Galyna Andrushko / Shutterstock; (timeline images from left to right) NPG 148 / National Portrait Gallery, from David Williamson, *The National Portrait Gallery History of the Kings and Queens of England*; duncan1890 / iStockphoto; Henry VII, British School, Oil on oak panel, Dulwich Picture Gallery; **79** (bottom) bioraven / Shutterstock; **80** (top) University of Leicester; (bottom) Reuters / Darren Staples; **81** University of Leicester; **83** (top) Colin Underhill / Alamy Stock Photo; (bottom) University of Leicester / Carl Vivian; **84** (top left) David Hughes / Shutterstock; (top right) markgoddard / iStockphoto; (helmet) Artur Balytskyi / Shutterstock; **85** University of Leicester; **85** (skull illustration) Morphart Creation / Shutterstock; **86** (top) Jacek Wojnarowski / Shutterstock; (bottom) trabantos / Shutterstock; **87** (girl) Nataliya Turpitko / Shutterstock.

Chapter 6: 89 (Depiction of prehistoric humans of the Ice Age) Henning Dalhoff / Science Photo Library; **90** Sheila Terry / Science Photo Library; **92** Gaelfphoto / Shutterstock; **93** © Ministère de la Culture / Centre National de la Préhistoire; **94** (top) Stephane Bidouze / Shutterstock; (bottom) salajean / Shutterstock; **95** thipjang / Shutterstock; **96** Andia / Alamy Stock Photo / All Canada Photos; **97** thipjang / Shutterstock; **98** imageBROKER / Alamy Stock Photo; **99** Stéphane Jaillet (Édytem) – Équipe Chauvet – Ministère de la Culture et de la Communication; **100–101** (timeline background) Anthony Gibson / Unsplash; (timeline images from left to right) Ministère de la Culture et de la Communication; Ministère de la Culture et de la Communication; thipjang / Shutterstock; **100** (bear skull) Audrey Snider-Bell / Shutterstock; **102** (top) Ministère de la Culture et de la Communication; (centre) Ivoha / Alamy Stock Photo; (bottom) Ivoha / Alamy Stock Photo / All Canada Photos; **103** Stocktrek Images, Inc. / Alamy Stock Photo; **104** (top) © Patrick Aventurier – Caverne du Pont d'Arc; (bottom) Mark Hallett Paleoart / Science Photo Library; **105** (boy) cristovao / Shutterstock.

ACKNOWLEDGMENTS

I would like to thank my friend David Curtin, who first suggested the idea of a book about recent discoveries in archaeology and set me on a path of researching many fascinating finds.

Thanks also to the people at Annick Press for their encouraging response to the idea and for all the insights they contributed to improve it, and to Rivka Cranley at Annick, who ushered the book through its later stages to final form.

Many thanks, once again, to editor Catherine Marjoribanks for her supportive and constructive advice on the manuscript as it evolved.